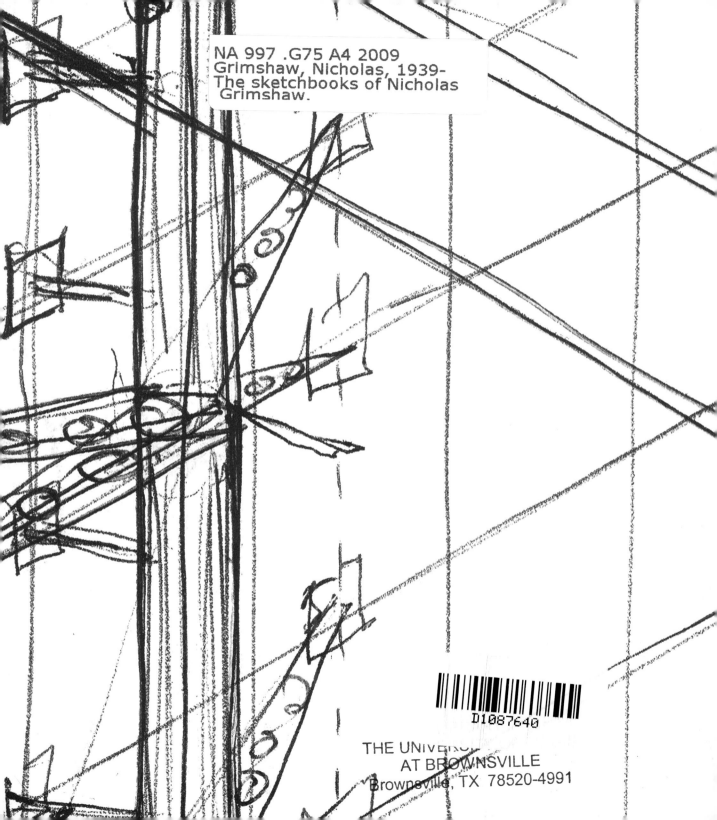

THE SKETCHBOOKS OF
NICHOLAS GRIMSHAW

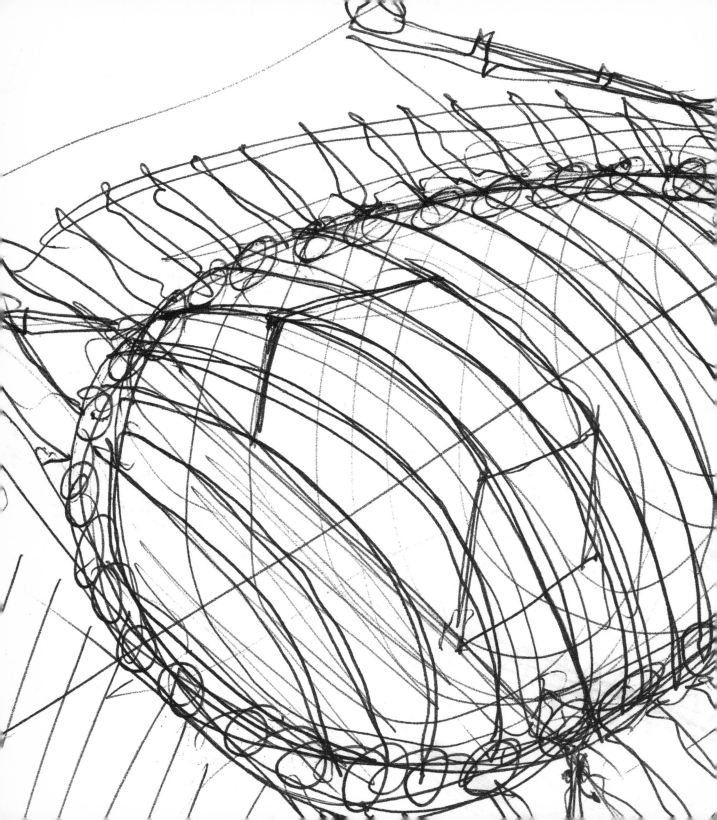

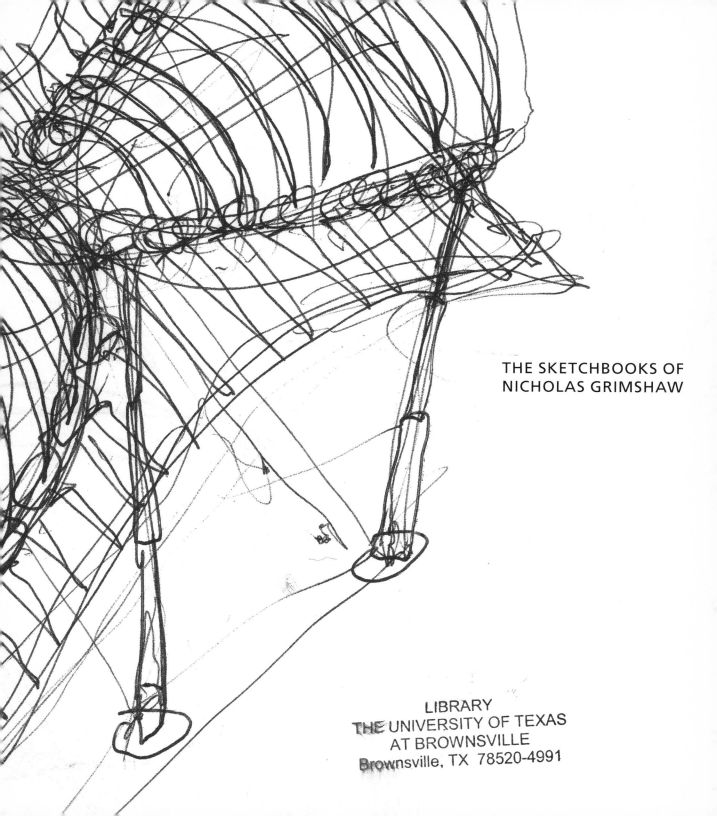

THE SKETCHBOOKS OF
NICHOLAS GRIMSHAW

First published on the
occasion of the exhibition
'CAPTURING THE CONCEPT:
The Sketchbooks of Sir Nicholas
Grimshaw CBE PRA from 1982
to 2007', held at Wimbledon College
of Art, the Royal Academy of Arts
and Edinburgh College
of Art, 2009–10

Published by the Royal Academy
of Arts in association with
The Centre for Drawing at
the University of the Arts London
and Edinburgh College of Art

GENERAL EDITOR
Stephen Farthing RA

ROYAL ACADEMY PUBLICATIONS
Lucy Bennett
David Breuer
Carola Krueger
Sophie Oliver
Peter Sawbridge
Nick Tite

COLLECTION AND
PHOTOGRAPHIC COORDINATION
Dominique Jenkins

BOOK DESIGN AND REPRODUCTION
Isambard Thomas, London

Printed in Italy by Graphicom

Copyright © 2009
Royal Academy of Arts, London

British Library Cataloguing-
in-Publication Data
A catalogue record for this book is
available from the British Library

ISBN 978-1-905711-62-8

Distributed outside the
United States and Canada
by Thames & Hudson Ltd, London

Distributed in the United States
and Canada by Harry N. Abrams, Inc.,
New York

ACKNOWLEDGEMENTS
We would like to acknowledge
the generous assistance of Michelle
Drew, Wendy Short, Anita Taylor
and Ed Webb-Ingall in the making
of this book.

ILLUSTRATIONS
ENDPAPERS:
detail of sketch for Financial Times
Print Works, page 31

PAGES 2–3:
detail of sketch for EMPAC, page 100

PAGES 16–17:
detail of sketch for British Pavilion,
Expo '92, Seville, page 40

PAGES 112–13:
detail of sketch for Eden Project,
page 75

PAGE 120:
detail of sketch for Lisbon Expo,
page 67

The sketches in this catalogue have not been chosen because they are particularly good drawings. They have been deliberately selected because they seemed to capture the 'spirit of the moment'. The projects covered here are all ones with which I have been particularly involved in the early concept stages. However, it takes a dedicated team to produce a building and I would not want for one minute to claim that my ideas alone have driven these projects to fruition.

As far as my own method of working is concerned, it is my habit to develop ideas in my head, in the shower, walking across the park, or maybe at a concert of particularly moving music, where I feel I have been 'transported' to another plane. At a certain moment the concept seems to need to travel down to my hand, which then operates my ballpoint pen. These sketches are the result.

Of course, I must acknowledge the creative work of all my friends and colleagues (both architects and engineers alike) who have contributed to these projects. And it is with the greatest humility that I put forward these personal sketches.

I have been hugely encouraged by Stephen Farthing, Rootstein Hopkins Professor of Drawing at the University of the Arts London, in this enterprise. The aim is to promote the idea that all who can, should get their concepts onto paper – in whatever medium – so that others can share them.

Sir Nicholas Grimshaw

NICHOLAS GRIMSHAW'S DRAWING BOOKS: TRANSLATION INTO BLUE LINES

Stephen Farthing

Sketchbooks, notebooks, journals and ship's logs are all places beyond the study, the studio, the map room and the laboratory in which, during both physical and creative journeys, inquisitive and creative people record their immediate observations, thoughts and ideas. At one end of the spectrum is the ship's log, whose primary purpose is to document a journey; at the other is the artist's sketchbook, used in the field before photography and since to record images that may prove useful back in the studio. Somewhere in the middle is the notebook, simply a portable workspace for recording and developing ideas and also for more mundane information such as shopping lists and telephone numbers.

To my mind Nicholas Grimshaw's drawing books sit quite comfortably between the ship's log and the sketchbook. They are clear and reliable enough to enable you to retrace his voyage from the evidence on the page. Full of inventions, lists and private thoughts, they are clearly not intended for public consumption. And their comparatively large size makes slipping them into the pocket out of the question. As logs of not simply an architectural career but a creative journey, they are extremely important documents for anyone interested in exploring both Grimshaw's architecture and the relationship between problem-solving and creativity.

When Grimshaw explains work-related concepts he often draws what he is talking about for you as he speaks. Drawing more slowly than you might imagine, pausing from time to time to let his pen catch up, he seems almost to be engraving the developing image onto a sheet of metal. It is not so much that he presses hard with his ballpoint pen (his preferred drawing instrument), rather that it takes him a while to form the image on paper. I suspect that this is his acknowledgement of the fact that his hand can, if he lets it, move faster than his thought process. When he draws you have a sense of him being in control.

Each of Grimshaw's drawing books was manufactured by Daler. They all started life with the same black cover and contained the same fairly smooth off-white drawing paper. With the exception of the first, which is A5 and thus pocket-sized, the books are all A4, i.e. 210 × 297 mm. In each he has drawn with a pen that he might easily have designed himself. Looking rather like the handle of a dental probe, his aluminium Rotring has faceted sides and delivers medium blue ink.

Grimshaw completes on average two books per year. You get the impression as you flick through these books that drawing in them is simply a part of life for him, and neither a treat nor a duty. Each book has taken its turn to travel with him; generally, however, he sits and draws in them at his desk at his practice in Clerkenwell.

When viewed as a group, the drawing books exude an uncanny sense of order, as if their purpose has never changed. It is not simply that they are all the same size, or that they have been rebound in the same cloth, or that they have been drawn by the same hand, even with the same type of pen, but rather that Grimshaw's primary interests have remained very much the same over some thirty years.

Drawn in January 1982, the first image reproduced here shows a carefully rendered, heavily annotated series of details of an industrial cladding system that Grimshaw devised for the Herman Miller Building in Chippenham. The last to be reproduced here (Book 63), drawn in late May or early June 2007, is a sketch for the roof of Pulkovo Airport in St Petersburg, which has pasted alongside it a list headed 'St Petersburg – Influences': 'Low Sun (glints) – Snow/Ice – Gold – Hot Summer/Cold Winter…' Writing about this drawing, Grimshaw remarks: 'The roof shapes were based on the idea of retaining the snow as insulation and allowing it to melt slowly *in situ*. Small roof lights allowed shafts of low winter sunlight to reflect from small areas of gold surface within the roof space.'

Grimshaw's drawing books are a place in which words, images, maps and calculations work together not only to solve problems, but also to sift and develop new ideas. Spread across pages 56 and 57 of Book 8 is an extraordinarily dense cluster of information related to the Scottish National Aquarium project in Broomielaw, Glasgow: a fairly hurriedly drawn section cantilevered out over the River Clyde, with the river's high- and low-tide levels drawn in; a pasted-in photocopy of a map of the site with Grimshaw's proposal drawn over it in plan; and finally, some calculations and information related to projected visitor numbers – all this for a gallery yet to be built. On these two pages alone we can see how a good draughtsman and designer uses mathematics,

cartography, collage and text to build a drawing and design a building.

In stark contrast, Grimshaw's early sketch for the Eden Project, an extremely simple and elegant image, sits on page 17 of Book 46 with plenty of white space around it. It is as if he made this drawing to record an already clearly formed idea and in the process gave it the space he knew it deserved. The Eden Project drawing is in no sense speculative or tentative. It is a complete concept laid out in line, then fully explained by just four words: 'pipes, fork-lift access'. The drawing immediately conveys the idea of a concealed central focal point containing the guts and a floating roof, free of services and support; like a fully functional wheel that has no spokes and an invisible hub.

Grimshaw believes in 'never redrawing the same thing more carefully' and that each page 'should be immediate'. As a result there is little evidence in any of his drawing books of either erasure or deletion. One interesting and effective exception turns up on page 103 of Book 16, in a drawing that tries out an idea for the roof of the British Pavilion at the Seville Expo '92. Here there is an uncharacteristic final 'tidying-up': Grimshaw uses Tipp-Ex correction fluid to obliterate some early structural lines in order to enhance the more organic rhythms of his conclusion.

What becomes clear as you work your way through these books is the degree to which Grimshaw has become increasingly interested in the lyrical and big, generous flowing shapes that elegantly demonstrate the essentials. On page 11 of Book 51, for example, the shape of the roof of the Frankfurt Trade Fair Hall is made with just two lines, just like the Copenhagen Bridge on page 25 of Book 61. As the books progress they reveal a mind moving over time from a preoccupation with detail to an engagement with the bigger picture.

Perhaps the most important aspect to reflect on in this brief exploration of Grimshaw's drawing books is their purpose. Unlike many sketchbooks and drawing books, they contain few images drawn from the visible world. There is no evidence of Grimshaw sitting at a window sketching the view, of holidays overseas, or of him sifting natural forms in search of stimulus. They contain neither distractions nor sub-plots: just a steady flow of drawings that relate directly to a controlled design process.

When you consider the lack of torn-out pages and erasure it seems likely that most of Grimshaw's thinking was done some time before he put pen to paper. If this is the case, what he gives us on paper is the visualisation of ideas not made through drawing but modified by the act of drawing. The mysterious process of visualising and modifying images in the mind – an activity that I suspect Grimshaw is not only good at but better at than most – can best be described as cerebral drawing, and it precedes the physical act.

Grimshaw's drawing books are a reservoir of structures, concepts and appearances that he has constructed in his mind and then translated into blue lines. These blue lines bridge the gap between cerebral images and spoken words, becoming an elegant beginning to a lengthy process of development. The contents of his drawing books are designed to prompt scores of larger, more finished, more detailed, more measured, less estimated, computer-generated drawings – all of which are printed, read, corrected and revised in their turn. It is only when these drawings are complete that the blue lines become metal and glass.

HUMANISING TECHNOLOGY

Peter Davey

Nick Grimshaw has always been fascinated by technology. As a student at Edinburgh College of Art, he impressed the rest of us by incorporating the latest developments like hyperbolic paraboloids and Buckminster Fuller domes in his second-year designs. Damnably difficult to draw and calculate, such elements (which have sometimes cropped up later in his work) seemed unforced, and it was natural that he should become associated with the avant-garde Archigram movement when he moved to London to complete his studies at the Architectural Association, then the most daring and adventurous architectural school in the world.

At the AA, Grimshaw picked up some topical concerns. For instance, his final thesis was a proposal for an urban university set in Covent Garden on a 125-acre site assembled by the GLC. Thank goodness the GLC never proceeded with their planned demolition, for it would have wiped out one of the most dearly loved bits of central London. Comprehensive redevelopment of the area may have been utterly wrong, but Grimshaw learned much from his project – principally perhaps that it is possible to generate an overall order, a grid to cope with the main demands of a brief, while allowing flexibility to cope with particular exigencies of site and the changing demands of individuals.

Another inheritance from student days is Grimshaw's devotion to understanding how buildings work. One of his most memorable AA submissions was his analysis of a vernacular Greek windmill that, unlike the meticulously measured renderings of monuments normally produced for such exercises, carefully and dramatically investigated the ways in which the mechanism worked. The drawings were remarkably free but confident, in style similar to the way in which Grimshaw draws by hand today. Lines may have been wobbly in places, but they were confident and clearly explained how the wooden cogs, spars and shafts related to each other. From this traditional timber building, Grimshaw learned much about principles of prefabrication and replaceability of parts, and later applied these to construction in glass, metal and plastic.

All three materials were used in Grimshaw's first built project, a service tower for a student hostel in Sussex Gardens, Paddington. Six Victorian terraced houses had been acquired by the client to be converted into accommodation for 200 students. Modern services were needed, so Grimshaw designed a tower in the houses' back gardens that contained bathrooms, lavatories and launderettes. The building was almost completely prefabricated, and its construction was revolutionary. A hollow slender steel column was swiftly erected and acted as a crane that swung other components into position. Such integration of services and structure was to become a hallmark of Grimshaw's career. Each bathroom unit was prefabricated in glass-reinforced plastic (GRP) by a firm that normally made boats. Even in this first building, Grimshaw (an ardent sailor) showed how the inventiveness and economy of nautical design can be an inspiration for building.

So tightly were the units packed that the tower was nicknamed the 'Corncob'. It became widely influential – few architects have started their careers with such panache. Now, the tower has entered the realm of

architectural myth, for it was dismantled when the terrace was converted into an hotel. But Grimshaw learned much from the experience of building it: for instance, how to choose manufacturers, sometimes not previously associated with building, and how to transfer their technologies to make totally new building elements. Prototyping and rigorously testing new components were disciplines little practised by architects, though common among product designers. Co-ordinating a large number of suppliers and subcontractors to a very rigorous and precise programme was another discipline learned at Sussex Gardens that has informed all Grimshaw's subsequent work.

Unlike traditionally constructed buildings, in which there is usually a good deal of overlap in the building sequence to allow for time-consuming setting and curing of wet materials, prefabricated ones are built rapidly so that delicate and complicated elements are not left lying around. On the whole, Grimshaw's work avoids wet and heavy building processes like brickwork and *in-situ* concrete (though concrete is often used in prefabricated components). From the beginning, Grimshaw's buildings have been lightweight, precise and finely honed.

Grimshaw is often categorised as a high-tech architect, like Richard Rogers and Norman Foster, and he has much in common with them. High-tech is, on the whole, a British architectural phenomenon which perhaps draws on the nation's nineteenth-century tradition of building in iron and glass, seen in the majestic train sheds of Victorian railway stations and the great conservatories like the Kew Palm House.

These relied on prefabrication, standardisation of parts and new materials like sheet glass and mass-produced cast iron. Another influence was Buckminster Fuller, the inventor of geodesic domes, very lightweight structures capable of long spans in all directions. Into this mix was stirred the example of the French architect and engineer Jean Prouvé, who in the first half of the last century developed forms of industrialised cladding in steel and aluminium.

In theory, high-tech could provide extremely flexible buildings, quickly and at moderate cost. At first, such work appeared without reference to its surroundings on green-field or run-down isolated urban sites. Well-mannered boxes like the Herman Miller Assembly Plant at Bath developed GRP construction further and provided remarkably flexible spaces that could be varied by interchanging opaque panels with transparent panels and doors; internal partitions could be shifted easily; windows and doors could be placed anywhere on the perimeter. Alterations could be undertaken quickly by maintenance staff without having to call in a builder. By imposing overall geometric discipline, Grimshaw was able to give his client much freedom to rearrange the factory as manufacturing and management techniques changed.

The approach was developed further in the British headquarters for BMW at Bracknell, a building whose panels consisted of two aluminium skins with a dense polyethylene core; joints were made with neoprene zipper gaskets. Aluminium was chosen rather than GRP because it can be recycled – an early instance of the ecological awareness that has increasingly influenced

Grimshaw's work. The same white finished panels were used in both the big warehouse and the office block, giving visual continuity between the two very different parts of the complex.

A silver finish was chosen for the cladding of the Oxford Ice Rink (this time a development of panels originally intended for cold-storage buildings). A column-free space was obviously essential, so the main roof loads were transferred to a central spine beam and from there by stainless-steel rods to two 30-metre tall masts, one at each end of the building. The arrangement greatly reduced the need for piling in the marshy ground, while the dramatic outline of the structure against the sky signalled the presence of an important new public building. Known locally as the 'Cutty Sark', the building became an urban landmark and proved to be remarkably popular.

At this stage of Grimshaw's career, the geometric discipline and scale of his work was largely derived from industrial priorities. Since then, particularly as the location of many projects became more urban, scale became a reflection on context as much as on the process of manufacture. For instance, Sainsbury's in Camden Town, London, was one of the first supermarkets to be built in a densely developed chunk of inner city. The project required many innovations, not least in dealing with customers' vehicles. Rather than spreading cars around the store on acres of asphalt, as happens in suburban and semi-rural superstores, Grimshaw created a basement car park that he linked to the ground-floor sales hall by ramped travelators, onto which trolleys lock and unlock automatically – quite a

common device now, but one that in 1988 seemed revolutionary, offering possibilities of taming a previously maverick and destructive building type.

Above ground, the supermarket looks completely different from any other. The shallow curved roof of the sales hall is supported on each side by cantilevered steel supports that are prevented from toppling inwards over the roof of the hall by bundles of tie rods that demonstrably transfer the tensile loads to the ground. Upper floors on each side of the hall are propped on the cantilevers. They give the building roughly the same height as the surrounding early nineteenth-century brick terraces, and the clusters of ties give a rhythm to the long street elevation that echoes domestic scale.

In Berlin, Grimshaw faced a similar problem when the practice won the design competition for the Ludwig Erhard Haus, a headquarters for the Chamber of Trade and Commerce of the newly united city. Much accommodation was required on a comparatively small site on Fasanenstrasse, off the Kurfürstendamm, the centre of West Berlin. Hans Stimmann, the city architect, had a policy of preserving Berlin's nineteenth-century domestic scale of five- and six-storey city blocks. An innovative design that was sympathetic to this policy was developed, based on bridging the whole site with a series of arches from which the floors were hung, ensuring a flexible, column-free ground floor.

Because the site tapered in width, the arches varied in height, and seen from the back, the building is like a huge curving organic object that became known locally as the Armadillo. But on the Fasanenstrasse side, a six-storey vertical façade is created on the pavement edge,

articulated by bands of window with fritted glass
louvres to moderate the sun's heat. The façade and
its attic hide the curved back of the Armadillo from
the street. The stainless-steel clad arches are exposed
below the flat façade and terminate at pavement level
in huge hinges that incorporate cast stainless-steel feet
with claws. So an arcade is created under the arches with
a glass wall on its inner side that reveals the foyers and
public circulation of the interior. Two full-height atria
bring daylight into the middle of the building, and in
hot weather, flaps in the glazed roofs of the atria open
automatically to ventilate and cool the spaces
by convection.

From the first, Grimshaw has been fascinated
by long-span structures to create columnless spaces,
allowing users maximum freedom. In Frankfurt's famous
Messe complex, the Grimshaw practice was asked to
create a new trade-fair hall on one side of a large urban
square – the Agora. Boldly and counter-intuitively, the
practice decided to span the building over its 160-metre
length so that a continuous glazed elevation could be
presented to the Agora. A folded roof that combined
clearly distinguished tensile and compressive zones was
developed to cover the two storeys of exhibition halls.
Here, scale was completely different from that of
Camden Town, but the great hall sits dramatically
yet easily among its neighbours.

Zurich Airport is another very large building that
looks out over the world through a great glass wall. As
part of a consortium, Grimshaw was asked to design a
complex that would bring the disparate elements of a
rapidly growing airport together and, like the Oxford

Ice Rink and the Frankfurt Trade Fair Hall, act as an
icon for the whole enterprise. Completed in two stages
(landside and airside), the airport was built over a
mainline railway station from which escalators ascend
to check-in desks and a top level retail and restaurant
area. A great lens-like rooflight brings natural light
down to the lowest levels.

On the airside, light comes through the long glass
wall that faces runway and countryside and leans
backwards to avoid confusing reflections. It fronts the
vast departure hall that runs the whole length of the
building. Huge white A-frames of tubular steel support
the roof, which is made into a welcoming aerodynamic
form to greet incoming passengers. Into this tall space
are inserted two retail pods wrapped in cherrywood
veneer, warm notes in the otherwise austere white
volume.

The Georgian delicacy of Bath is very different
from Zurich Airport, Camden Town and Fasanenstrasse,
and when the practice was asked to create a new spa
complex for the city, there could be no question of a
dramatic contrast of materials. In Bath, the Roman and
Georgian elements were of course retained, but on the
site of a derelict 1930s municipal swimming pool,
a whole new collection of baths and steam rooms
was required, heated by the geothermal springs that
gave Bath its origin (and name).

A box of honey-coloured Bath stone is surrounded
by an outer glass box, so light pours into the interior
from three sides. The stone box rises above the glass
one to create an attic storey that relates in height to
the Georgian terraces on Bath Street. Grimshaw's new

British Pavilion, Expo '92,
Seville, interior view (left)

Eden Project, detail showing
the Core and biomes (right)

building fits into the existing complex matrix of
medieval and Georgian buildings with no fuss. Inside,
there is a large hot bath at the lowest public level where
people plash about under great mushroom-shaped
concrete columns. Above are changing and steam
rooms. The whole is topped off by another hot pool
on the roof, where you can loll in the open air even on
quite cold days and glimpse the Gothic pinnacles and
crockets of Bath Abbey through the steam.

Such a project clearly needed close control
of the temperature and humidity of the different
internal climates. Another dramatic experiment with
atmospheric management was the British Pavilion at
the 1992 Seville Expo. The city has the hottest climate in
Europe and has developed vernacular systems to make
buildings tolerable to live in, so its traditional fabric is
constructed around innumerable shady courtyards with
fountains dripping over moss and ferns. The latent heat
of evaporation cools the atmosphere without any need
for mechanical devices.

Grimshaw used similar principles, adapted to
industrial scale, in the pavilion, and these were
developed with engineers Ove Arup & Partners and
the water sculptor Bill Pye. The whole glass east wall
was constantly washed by water that, for the last five
metres, descended into a pool as a curtain of liquid
threads. Ample opportunities for evaporation were
offered by the arrangement, and the pumps that drove
the water were powered by solar energy collected in
photovoltaic panels incorporated in shading devices on
the roof. Further shading was provided by sheets of PVC-
coated polyester fabric (normally used in yacht sails)

attached to masts on north and south walls by details
derived from marine examples.

Shipping containers filled with water made
up the west wall to provide thermal mass. Almost all
the pavilion's elements had to be lightweight and
prefabricated in Britain. Mass endows buildings with
the ability to absorb heat by day and emit it at night –
hence the water that gave the containers thermal
capacitance. All these devices reduced the general
interior temperature from the virtually intolerable 40°C
outside to a much more agreeable 27°C. But in places
where many people congregated, for instance round
some of the audio-visual displays, localised mechanically
air-conditioned pods had to be provided to get the
temperature down to about 22°C. Even so, the short-
lived pavilion showed how the sun's energy could be
used in hot countries to cool buildings – lessons that
are only very gradually being understood and applied
in the tropics.

Another exhibition building concerned with
the environment is the Eden Project, built in a worked-
out china clay quarry in Cornwall. This visionary
scheme is intended to provide conservatories for
plants originating in different climates, and to be
a demonstration of low-energy building. In it, the
biggest greenhouse in the world is roofed not in
glass but in ETFE transparent plastic foil, a material
far lighter than glass. It is carried on geodesic 'biomes',
in which hexagonal grids of lightweight aluminium
struts support foil cushions containing air that acts as
heat insulation (it has been calculated that the biomes
are lighter than the air that they enclose). ETFE is also

Stainless-steel bracket used
in the International Terminal
at Waterloo

more or less self-cleaning, and can be repaired easily if it is damaged.

Other energy-saving innovations include the entrance block, where outer walls are constructed of rammed earth (a low-energy form of construction with high thermal mass traditional in southwest England); electricity is generated by a dedicated wind turbine and photovoltaic arrays, and irrigation water in the biomes comes from land drainage (mains water is used only for hand-washing and food preparation). Eden has proved immensely popular with public and staff as plants grow and change and new energy-conserving devices are added.

These days, virtually all architects express an interest in energy conservation and reducing carbon emissions. But few do so with the ingenuity shown at Eden and Seville.

Many preoccupations that have driven the practice from the first remain in the work. Grimshaw is often keen to let buildings show how they work (remember the Greek windmill). He celebrates joints and conjunctions, for instance in the stainless-steel pins and brackets in the glazed cladding of the International Terminal at Waterloo, which had to permit horizontal movement of 80 mm and vertical deflection of 6 mm as the enormously heavy trains moved in and out under the great glass roof. In the Financial Times Print Works at Wapping and the Western Morning News Headquarters and Print Works that hovers on a hillside above Plymouth, the ways in which the glass walls are hung and supported are immediately apparent. This fascination with connections extends to the smallest

scale. I remember once my glasses fell to bits and I was making a mess of putting them together. In a trice, Nick seized a jeweller's screwdriver and re-assembled them as good as new.

He has never had a trademark style. Nor has he succumbed to fashionable crazes. He is proud of the fact that more than 40 million people use his buildings every year and that 'most of these people find something to love'. He remains a committed Modernist and firmly believes that 'any site can accept a contemporary building, providing it is good enough'.

No matter how standardised the elements of which it is made, each building is honed by site, programme and context into being a particular three-dimensional statement about human needs and circumstances. Grimshaw is still as fascinated by technology as he was when he was a student. But in his work, technology is not an end in itself (as it is with some architects). His drawings show how he continuously adapts technology to serve humanity, and how his journey of exploration continues.

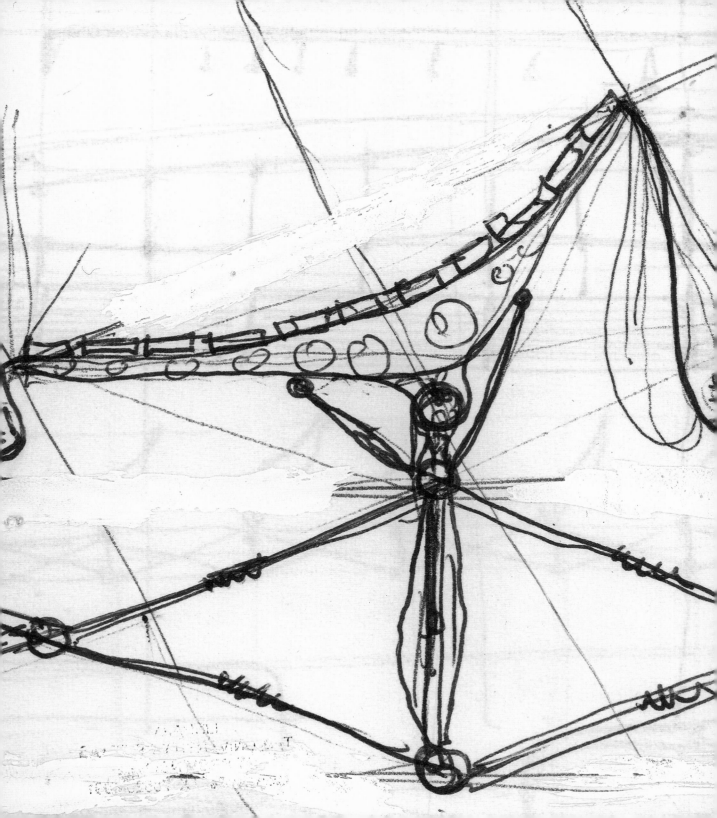

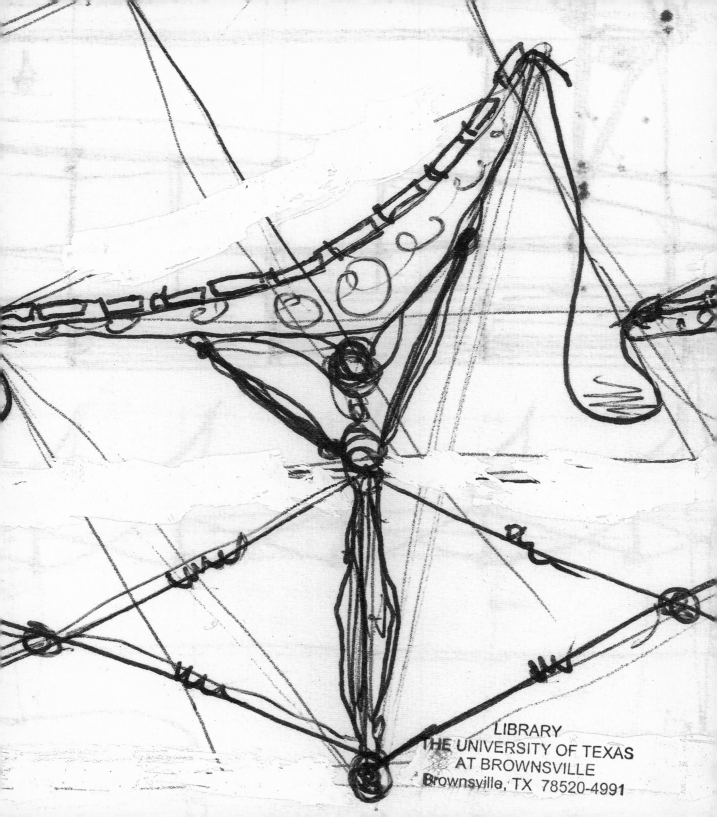

Here I was exploring
an incredibly cheap
industrial cladding
sytem – just one stage
up from 'wriggly tin'.

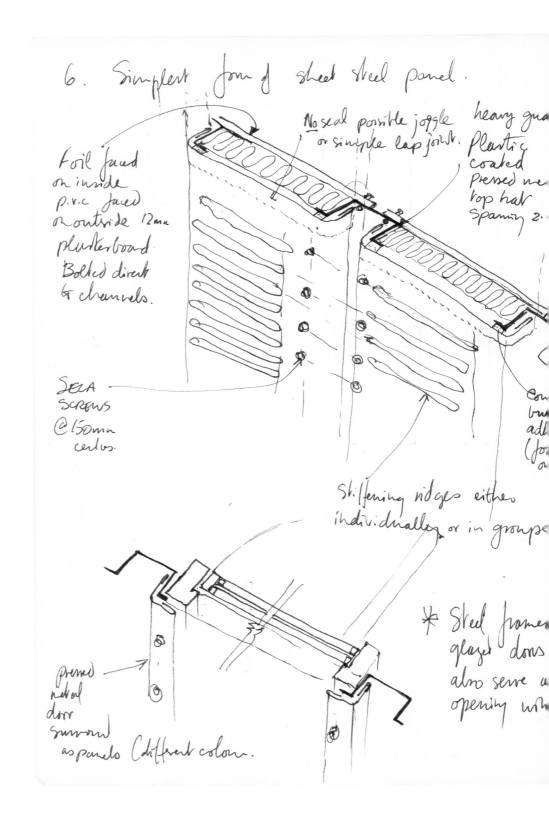

6. Simplest form of sheet steel panel.

Foil faced
on inside
p.v.c faced
on outside 12mm
plasterboard.
Bolted direct
to channels.

No seal possible joggle
or simple lap joint.

heavy gua[...]
Plastic
coated
pressed me[...]
top hat
spanning 2.[...]

SELA
SCREWS
@ 150mm
centres.

Stiffening ridges either
individually or in groups[...]

* Steel frame[...]
glazed doors [...]
also serve a[...]
opening wh[...]

pressed
metal
door
surround
as panels (different colour.

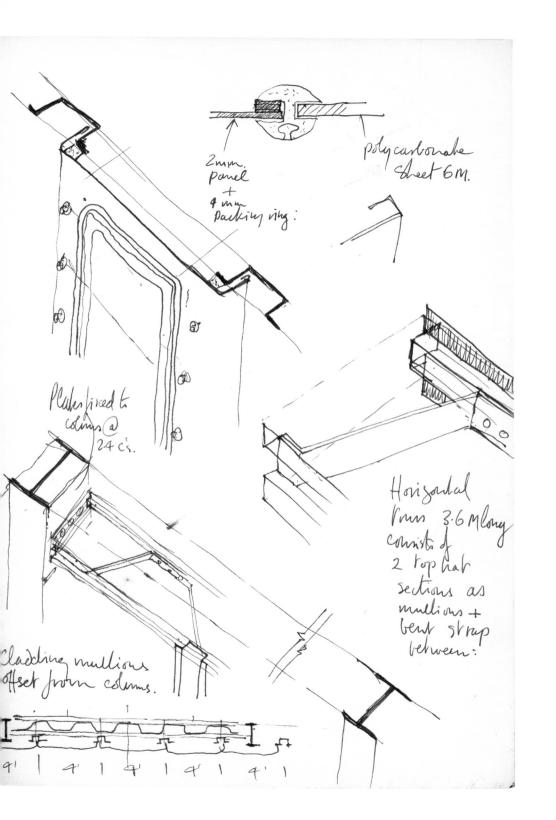

2mm.
panel
+
4 mm
Packing ring.

polycarbonate
Sheet 6M.

Plates fixed to
columns @
24 c's.

Horizontal
runs 3.6 M long
consists of
2 top hat
sections as
mullions +
bent strap
between.

Cladding mullions
offset from columns.

4' | 4' | 4' | 4' | 4' |

La Grande Arche,
La Défense, Paris

Book 3, pages 26–7
23 January 1983

A preliminary idea for the
competition for the site
which eventually became
'La Grande Arche',
centrepiece of the
financial district known
as La Défense.

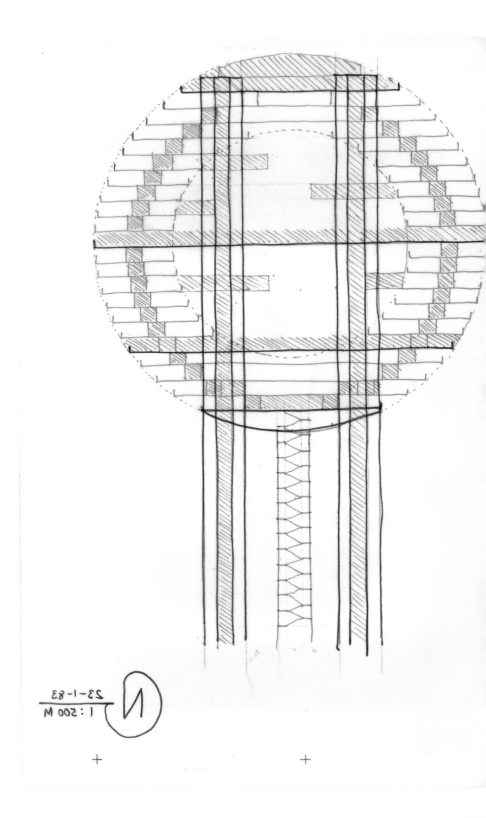

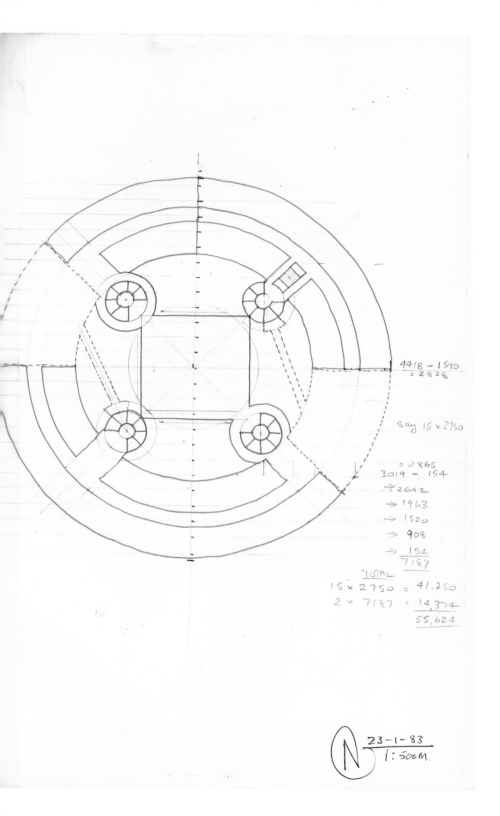

$$\frac{4918 - 1590}{= 2828}$$

Say 15×2750

$$= 2865$$
$$3019 - 154$$
$$\to 2642$$
$$\to 1963$$
$$\to 1520$$
$$\to 908$$
$$\to \underline{154}$$
$$\overline{7187}$$

TOTAL
$$15 \times 2750 = 41,250$$
$$2 \times 7187 = \underline{14,374}$$
$$\overline{55,624}$$

$$\frac{23-1-83}{1:500M}$$

Oxford Ice Rink

Book 4, pages 22–3
3 June 1983

A very early sketch exploring a masted structure with a central spine which is in turn supported by an extremely light insulated enclosure.

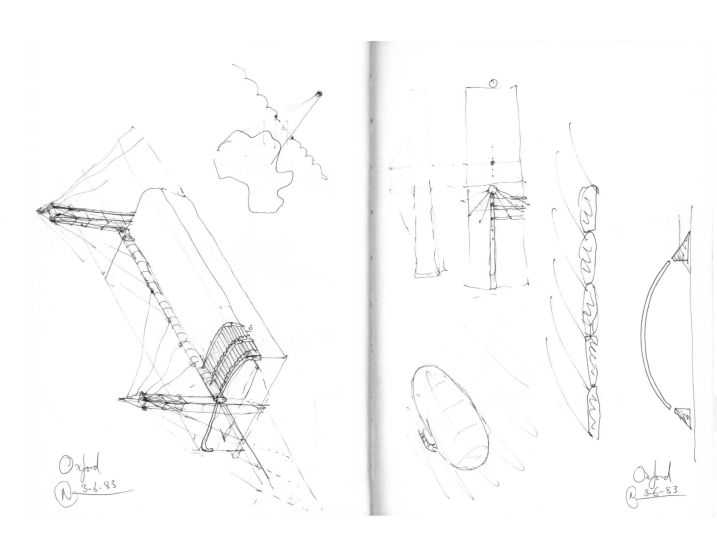

Oxford Ice Rink

Book 5, pages 76–7
c. October 1983

Details exploring how
hanging rods can be
adjusted in length as they
are gradually loaded.

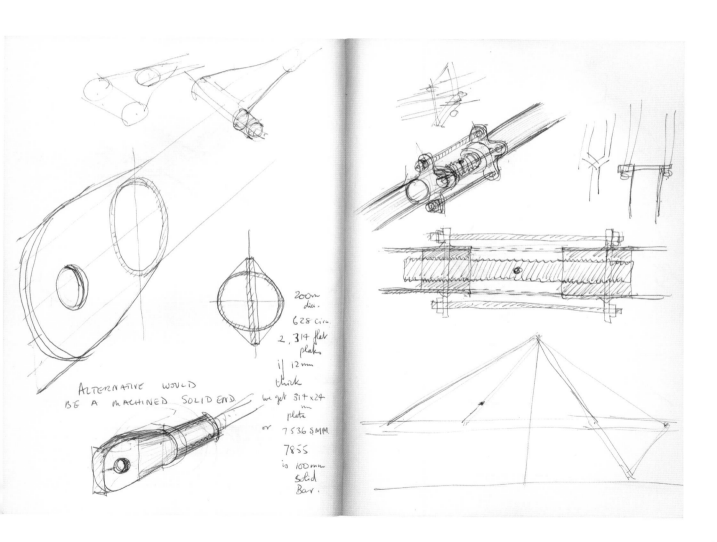

ALTERNATIVE WOULD
BE A MACHINED SOLID END

200m dia.
628 circ.
2,314 flat plaks
if 12mm thick
we get 314 x 24 mm plate
or 7536 SMM.
7855 is 100mm Solid Bar.

Ladkarn, Docklands,
London

Book 6, pages 98–9
c. April 1984

The brief for Ladkarn was
to create the cheapest
possible 'box' in which
to service heavy
construction vehicles.
This drawing shows two
simple volumes in large-
profile corrugated steel,
with rounded corners
softening the shapes.

The roof was held up by
trusses with a clear span,
which achieved a column-
free interior.

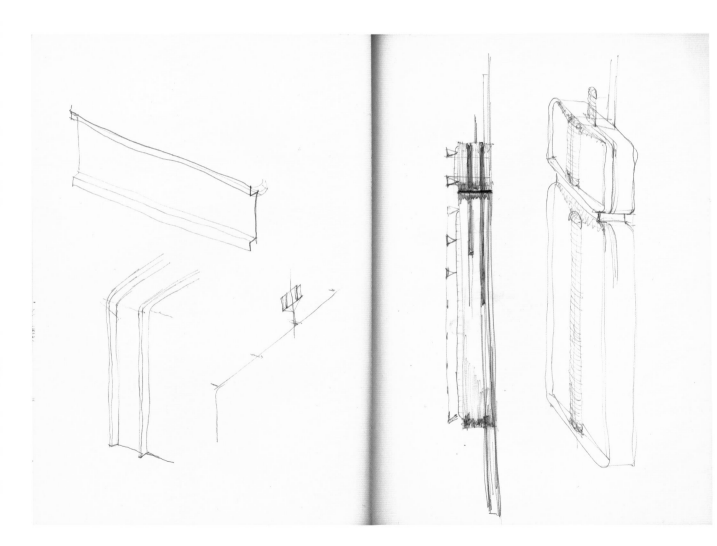

Oxford Ice Rink

Book 7, pages 52–3
c. October 1984

These mast details explore how a plate passed through the vertical mast in order to transfer the load from the hangar to the tie-downs.

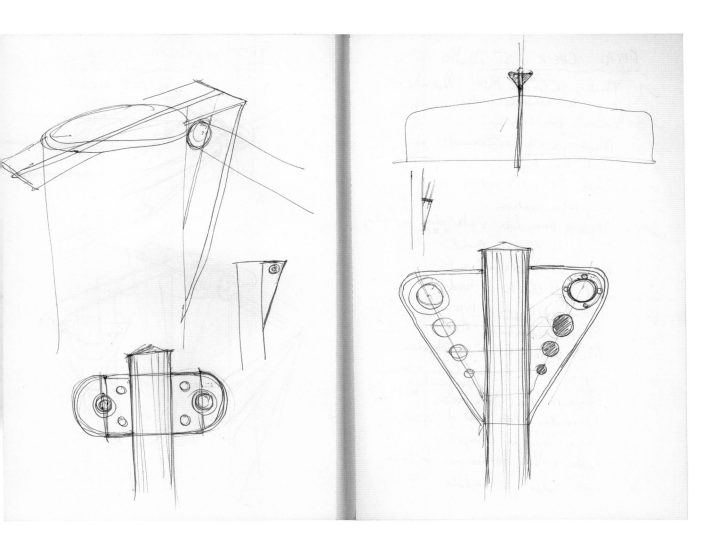

Book 8, pages 56–7
Late May/early June 1985

First thoughts for the
aquarium, a kind of oil-rig
structure cantilevered out
over the river bank.

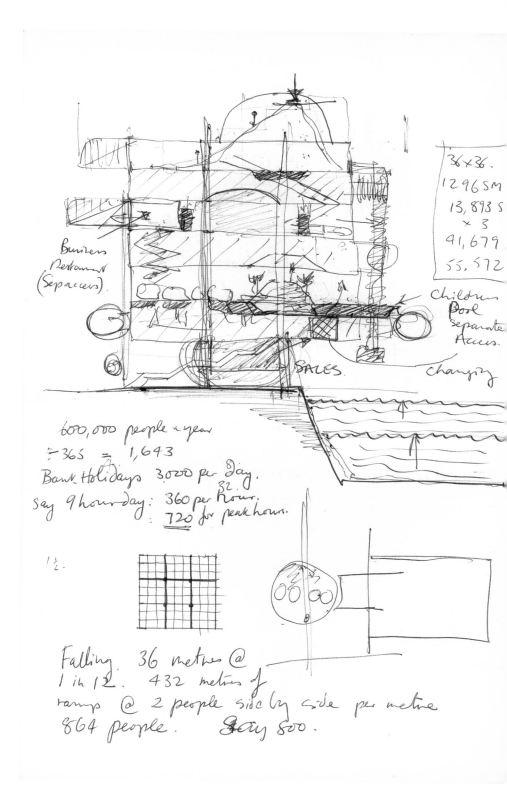

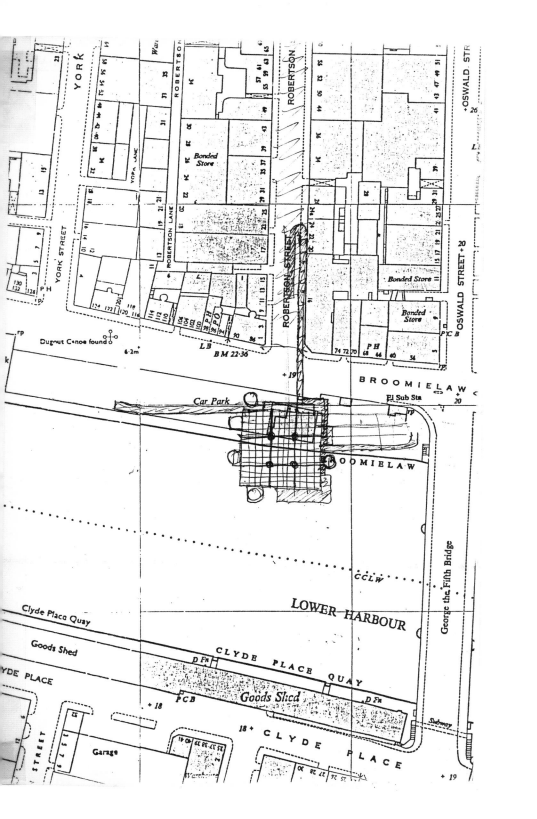

Sainsbury's Superstore,
Camden Town, London

Book 9, pages 42–3
Early December 1985

These initial drawings pay
particular attention to the
fire protection of the
steelwork. On the right,
a section of the building,
showing the proposed
basement car park.

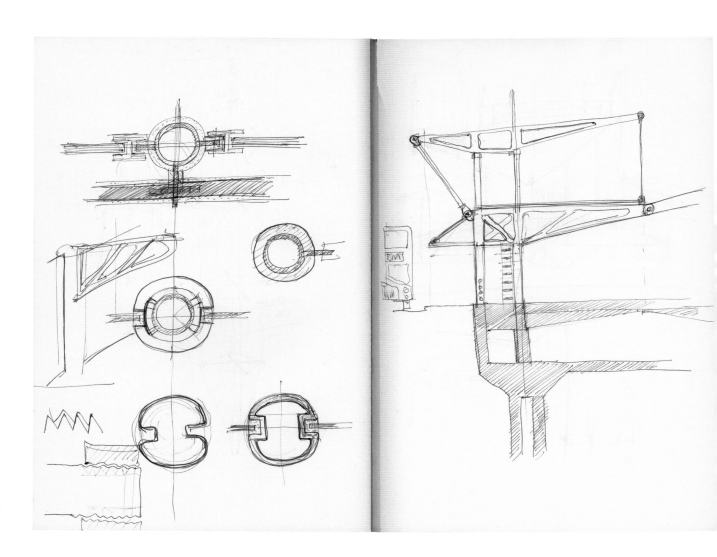

Homebase, Brentford, London

Book 10, pages 114–15
15 September 1986

The concept shown in these early sketches is a cable-supported 'fuselage' onto which a series of 'wings' are lightly propped at their extremities by a V-shaped structure.

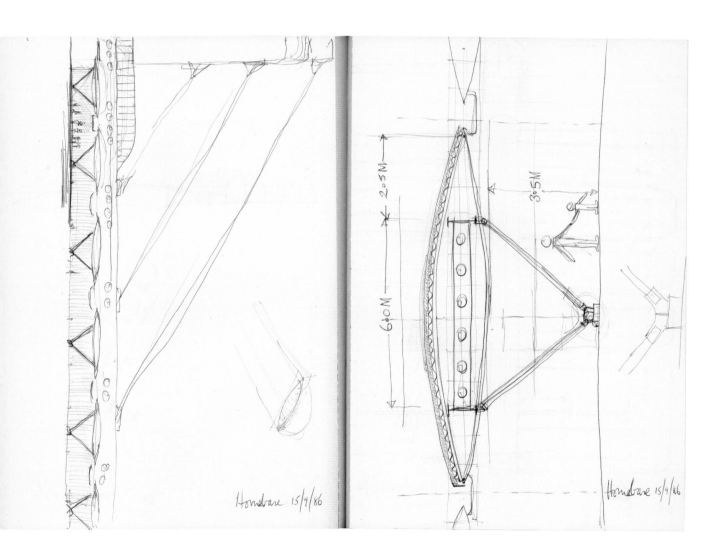

Homebase 15/9/86

Homebase 15/9/86

The exploratory sketch
on the right pursued the
idea that the structural
column would support
not only the roof beams
but also the glazed wall.
On the left, a sketch for
the Rank Xerox Research
Centre at Welwyn Garden
City, showing its big
horizontal louvres and
the way in which you
can see between them
whether standing
or seated.

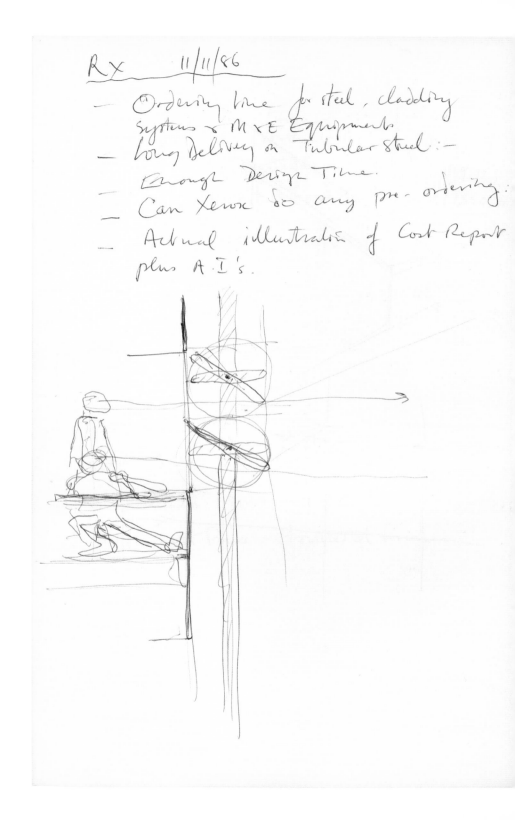

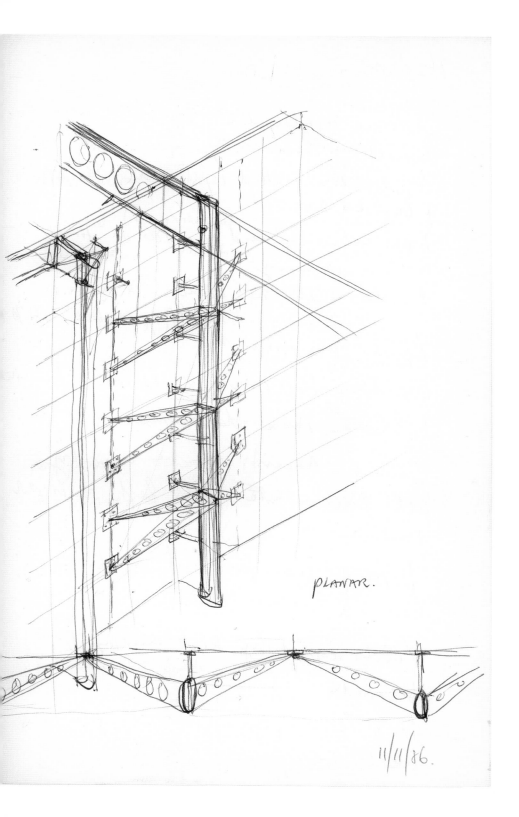

PLANAR.

11/11/86.

31

**Ladkarn, Docklands,
London**

Book 12, pages 131–2
27 August 1987

Concept sketches for an
office building. The site
was long and narrow
with a good view at
one end. I proposed two
blocks with a narrow
atrium between them,
affording glimpses of
the water to everyone.

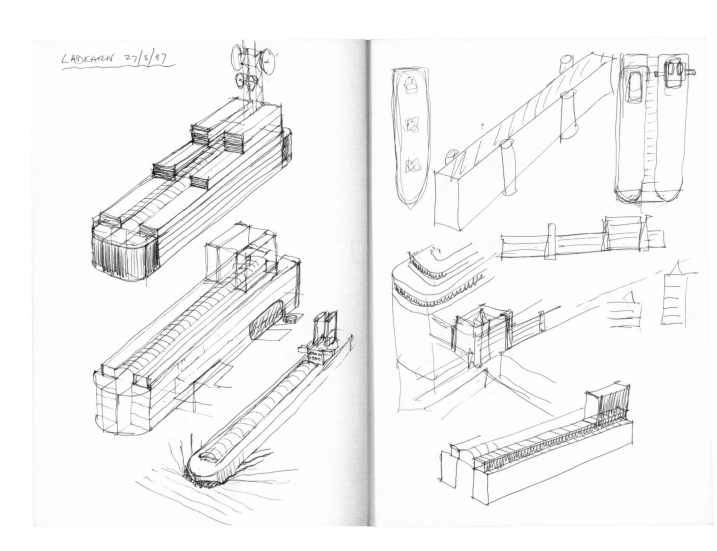

LADKARN 27/8/87

Slideshow

Book 13, pages 20–1
c. October 1987

Pictograms for a slide presentation in which I attempted to link industrial buildings, with their very basic materials and structures, to the new field of sports buildings.

12. Wiltshire Radio - Bathysphere?

13. SA.SH - Athletes Starting Blocks

14. H.M. Chippenham - Citroen Van.

15. Oxford Ice Rink - Radio Mast

16. Rank Xerox - Morphy-Richards Fan Heater

17. Ladkarn - Phase I - Cutty Sark.

18. B.M.W. - Motor Bike

19. Stock Bridge - Lubetkins Penguin Pool

20. Sainsbury's - A Bridge Forth Bridge? (Check Brunel Slides)

21. Homebase - Hipframe AXO

22. Financial Times - Americas Cup Cross Trees from Mast

23. Ladkarn - Dollar Bay - Aquarium?

International Terminal Waterloo, London

Book 14, pages 186 and 192
Early June 1988

An idea for two towers (irregular ellipses in shape) standing in front of the International Terminal. This grand entrance from York Road would have led over the roof to a new square above the domestic station.

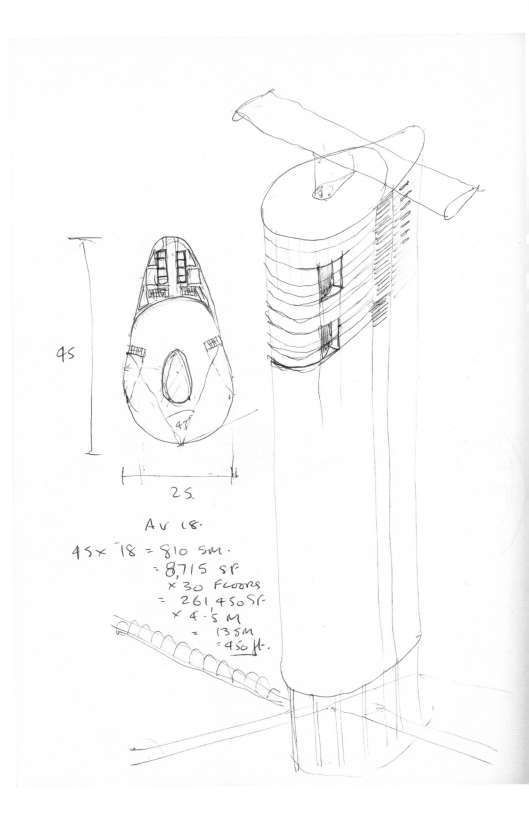

45

25

Av 18.

45 × 18 = 810 SM.
= 8,715 SF
× 30 FLOORS
= 261,450 SF
× 4.5 M
= 135 M
= 450 ft.

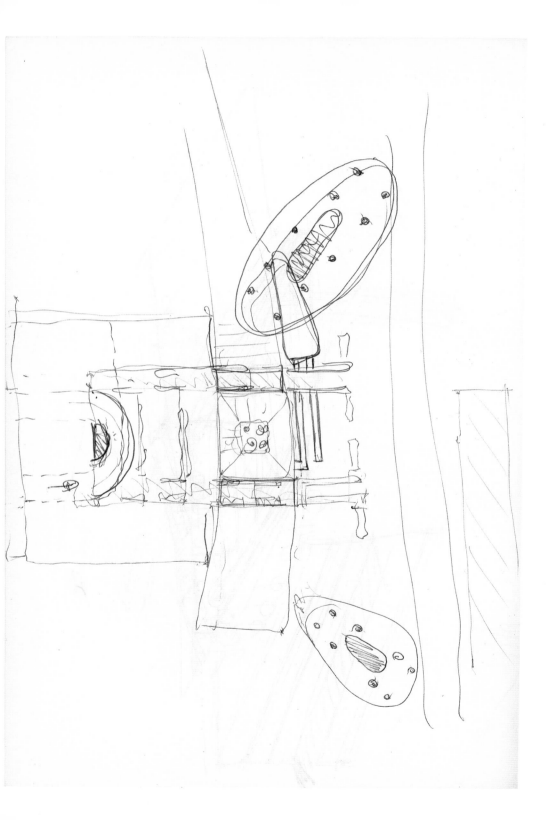

Book 15, pages 102–3
Early October 1988

This idea is based on the
curved steel arches that
were proposed at one
time for this project. The
arches support a totally
glazed enclosure which
can be cleaned by means
of the cradles shown here.

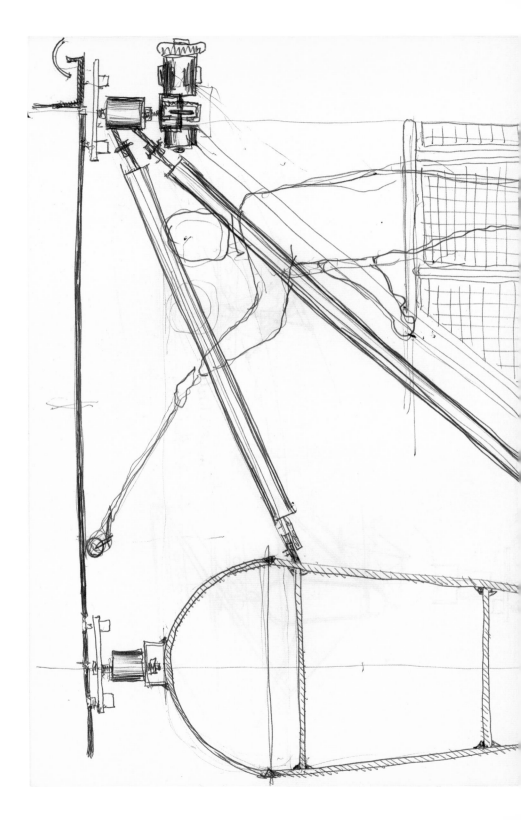

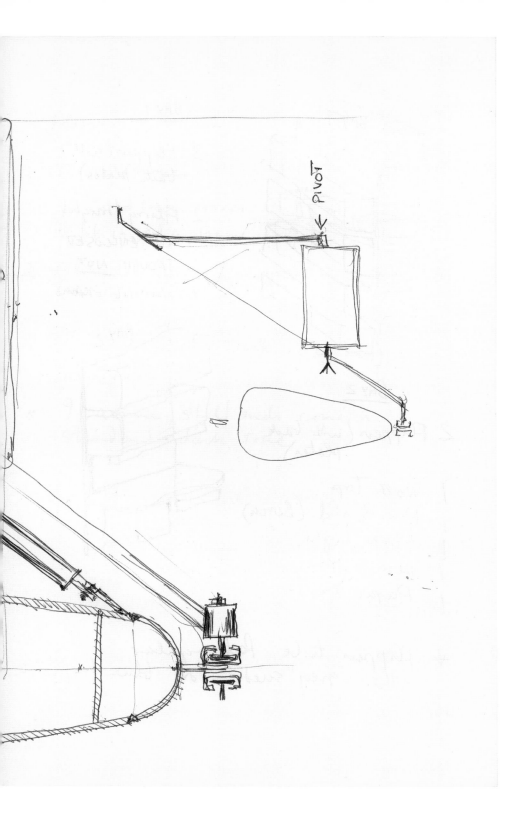

PIVOT

Preliminary ideas for
the Seville Pavilion
which already assume
'pods' for activities,
escalators for circulation
and a water wall for
cooling.

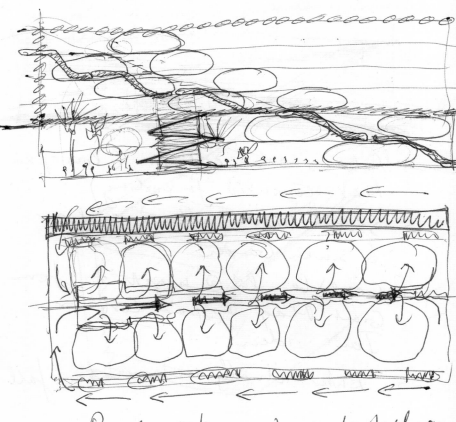

3. MOVEMENT OF PEOPLE OR THINGS

→ People enter under waterfall and
zig-zag through it to two
floors below to a sunken garden

→ Escalators take them to top & they
walk downwards through exhibits.

→ OR whole centre is giant
moving staircase passing between
exhibits

→ Individual Pods are air
conditioned but not whole environ

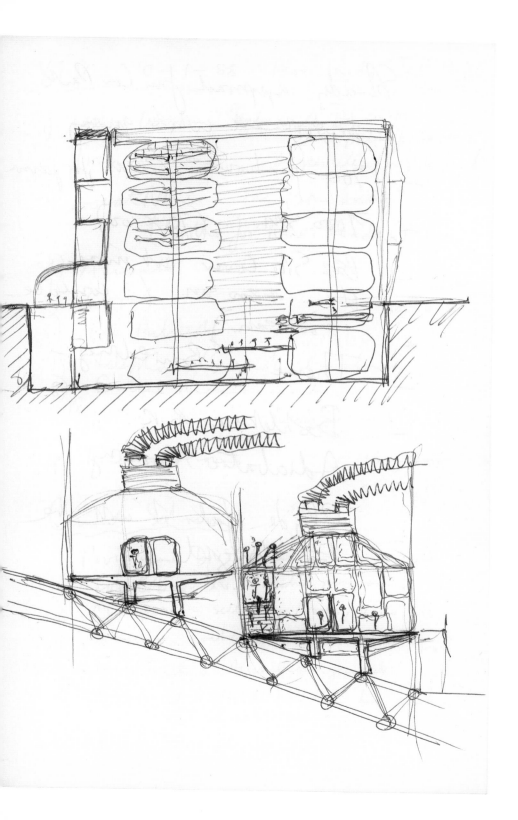

Book 16, page 103
14 January 1989

Book 19, page 105
17 October 1989

In this concept for the
roof, curved solar panels
are directly supported
by the roof trusses and
linked together by a
flexible membrane that
forms a trough for
collecting rainwater. The
sketch on the right shows
the idea of using water
tanks as a heat barrier on
the west wall, the water
wall on the east elevation
and solar cells on the
roof.

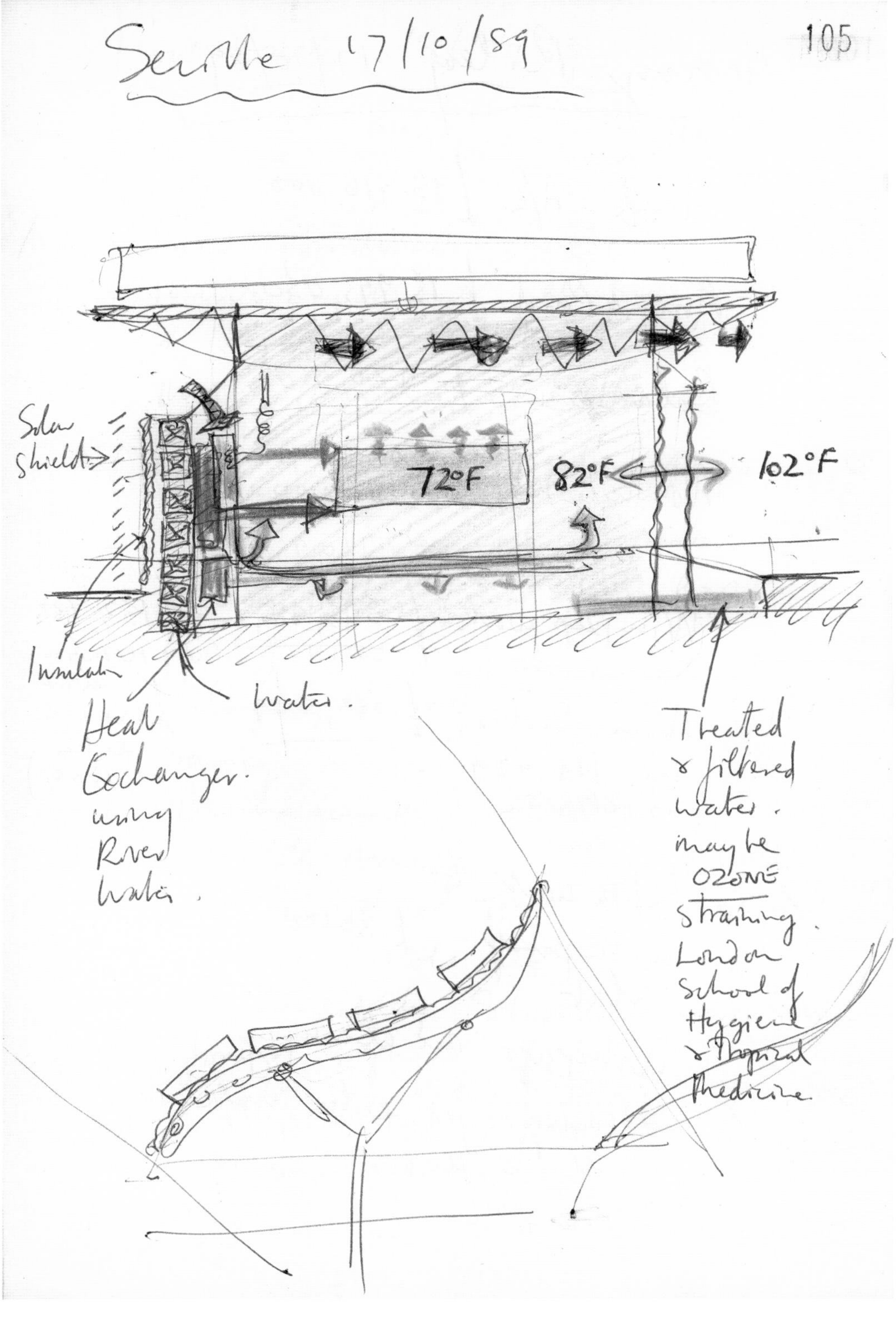
Seville 17/10/89
105
Solar shield
72°F
82°F
102°F
Insulation
Water.
Heat Exchanger. using River water.
Treated & filtered water. maybe OZONE straining. London School of Hygiene & Tropical Medicine

Heathrow Terminal 5, London

Book 17, pages 104–5
Late April 1989

In these preparatory sketches for the submission for Terminal 5, the concept assumes that a Westinghouse train (as used at Stansted) calls at all aircraft stands and that there is a very large terminal at each end of the airport.

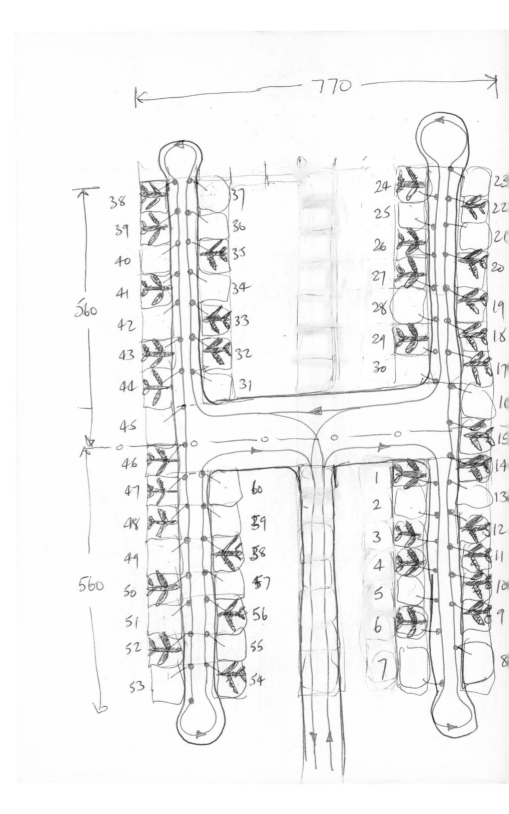

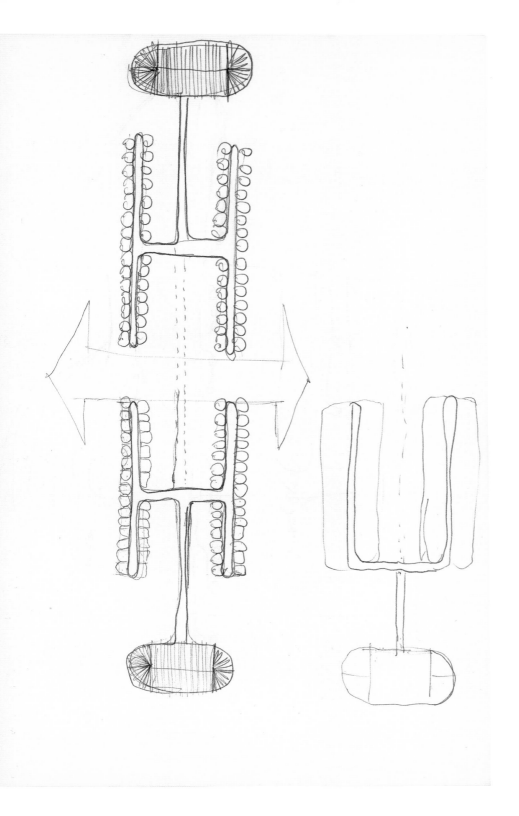

Bibliothèque nationale, Paris

Book 18, pages 108–9
21 June 1989

An early sketch for the competition for the 'Très Grande Bibliothèque' (now the Bibliothèque nationale). The concept is centred on a public-circulation spine with a view of a vast industrial book stack. Specialist libraries are accessed from the spine and reading areas are on the periphery.

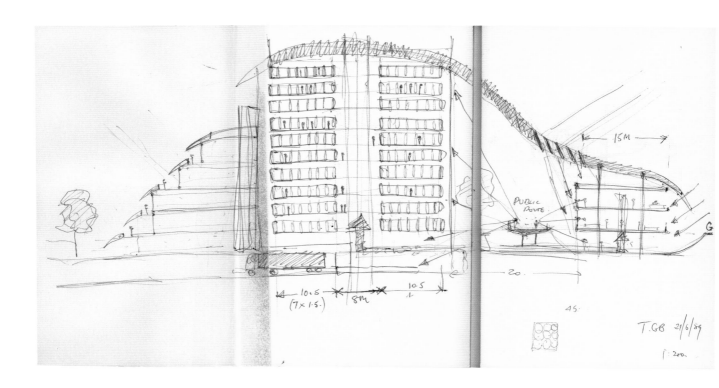

A concept making use
of the vertical space
above a work station,
thus enabling more
people to be
accommodated.

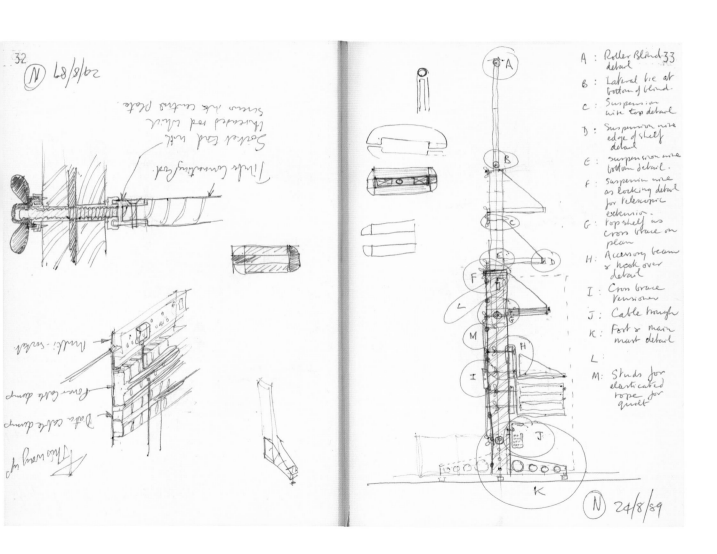

Book 21, pages 74–5
Late April 1990

This concept detail turned out to be an important forerunner to the final design of the roof. It allows adjustment to the angle of the mullions which are attached to the tubular structure. Thus the glazing panels can be adjusted in section and (with the help of a concertina gasket) in plan.

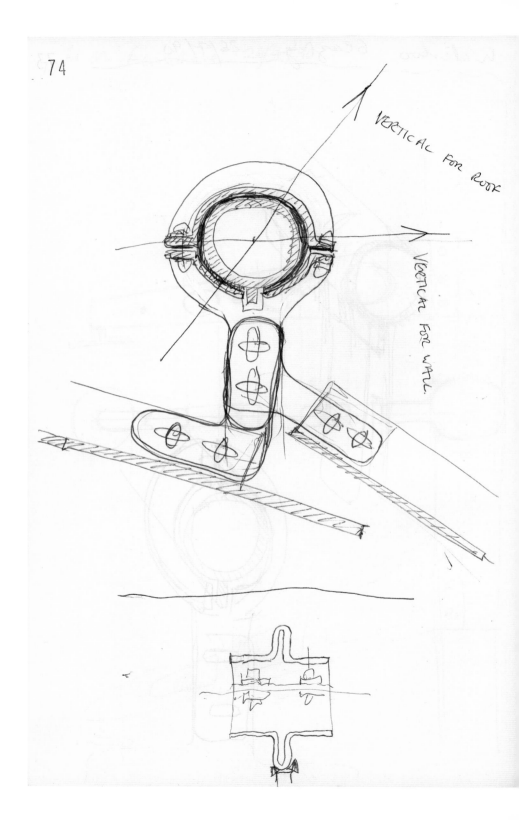

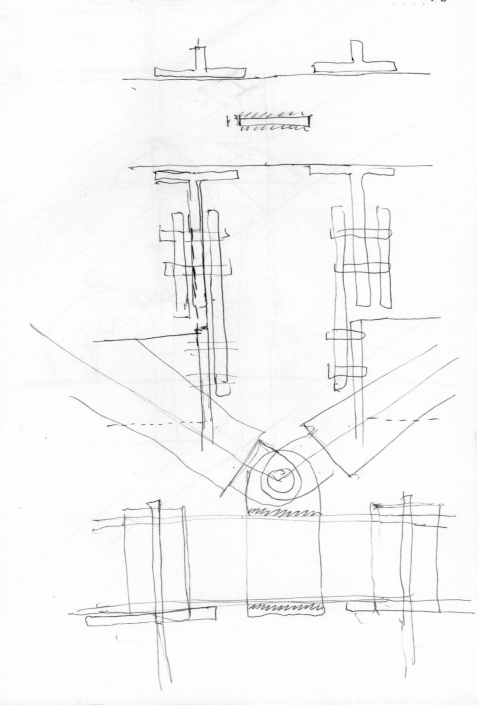

Igus Factory, Cologne

Book 21, pages 144–5
23 June 1990

In these preliminary
ideas for the Igus plastics
factory, masts support
the roof producing an
unimpeded column-
free interior space.
Hemispherical domes
in the roof include north-
facing roof lights that
give good natural
daylight to the factory
floor. The sketch on the
right refers to the 'Skylon'
at the 1951 Festival of
Britain, which I always
thought was an inspired
piece of design.

144

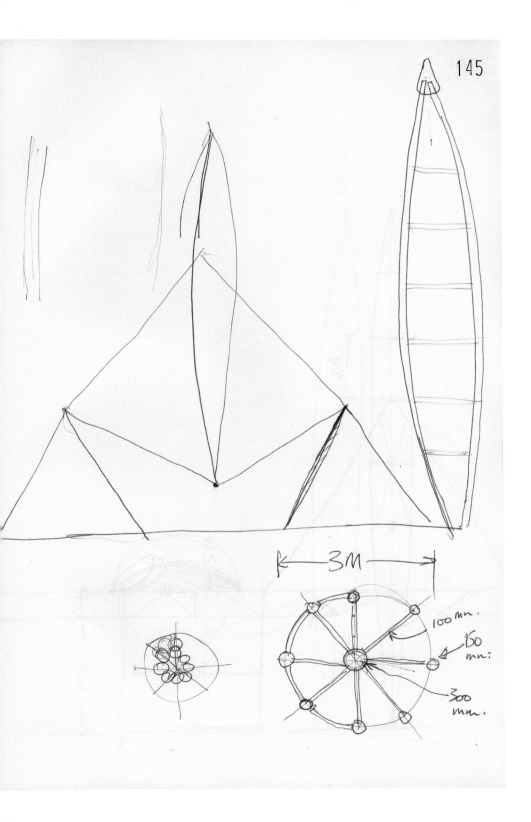

145

⊢— 3M —⊣

100 mn.

150 mn:

300 mn.

This drawing survives
from an early meeting
with Roland Paoletti,
chief architect of the
project, who was
sounding out options for
the extension. I was
strongly in favour of
standardisation and
proposed an 'extrusion'
for the platforms,
including platform
surfaces, seat lighting,
information panels and
possible supports for
sliding doors.

4

Jubilee Line.   5 July 1990
Roland Paoletti,   Andreas.
— Industrial Design Kit of Parts Team
    Seats   NGP (+ Jan + Roy Fleetwood)
Signage × electronic displays.
Advertising – illuminated
Lighting –
Ticket Windows: / Machines / Barriers.
Station Finishes: ⎤
Cleaning   ⎬
Waste Bins   ⎦
Handrails.
— Brief for each Station to be provided)
+ Costs
+ Programme
+ Civil Engineering Co-Ordination
Contract Method)
 — Station Contracts will be let on
    ICE Contracts administered)
    by L.T. Engineers.

5

Elimination rather than elaboration
— no hiding places for bombs.
— assume maintenance is bad.

NGP ...
Hopkins.
ABK.
McAslan :
DRU (Architeken Grupp U-BAHN)
Horden
L.R.T.
Ron Herron.
John Winter
Ian Ritchie.

Barn, Norfolk

Book 23, pages 66–7
28 January 1990

Sketches for a bridge
in the barn. The first-floor
accommodation is
suspended in the roof
space and three bridges
link the various rooms.

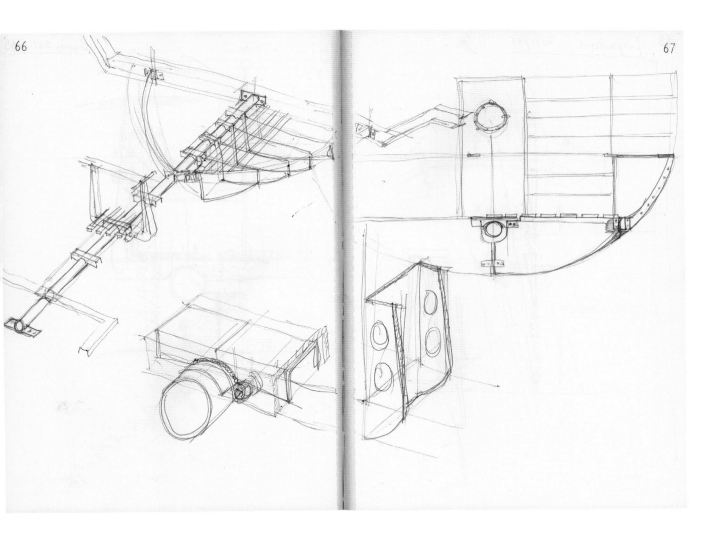

66

67

Book 23, pages 112–13
Early March 1991

This drawing explores the issue of movement in the x, y and z axes both at the column and at the face of the glass cladding. The 'arm' was cast in spheroidal graphite and the 'hand' was a lost wax stainless-steel casting.

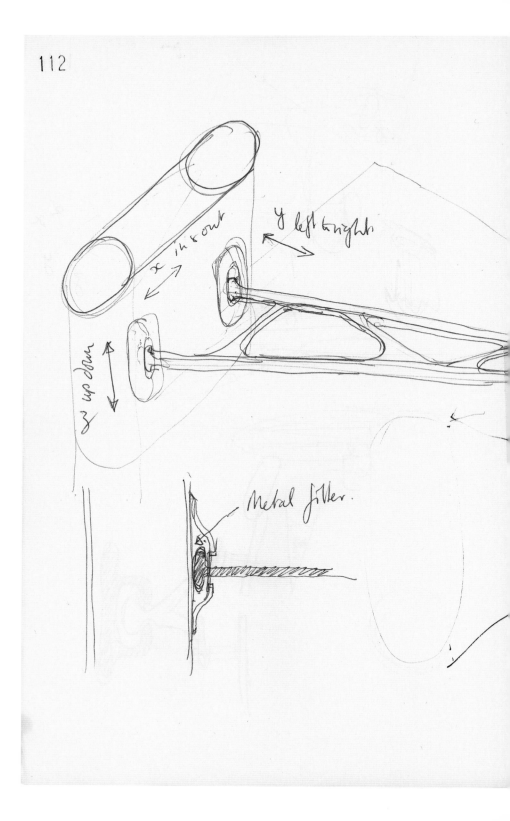

112

Metal filler.

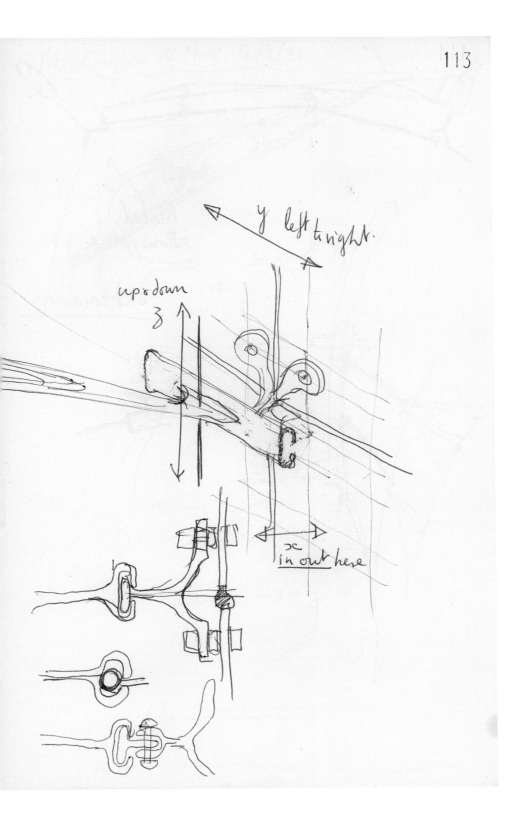

y left to right.

up o down
3

x
in out here

An initial sketch of the bony arched form of the Berlin Stock Exchange (eventually the Ludwig Erhard Haus). On the right, a checklist of points concerning the barn in Norfolk.

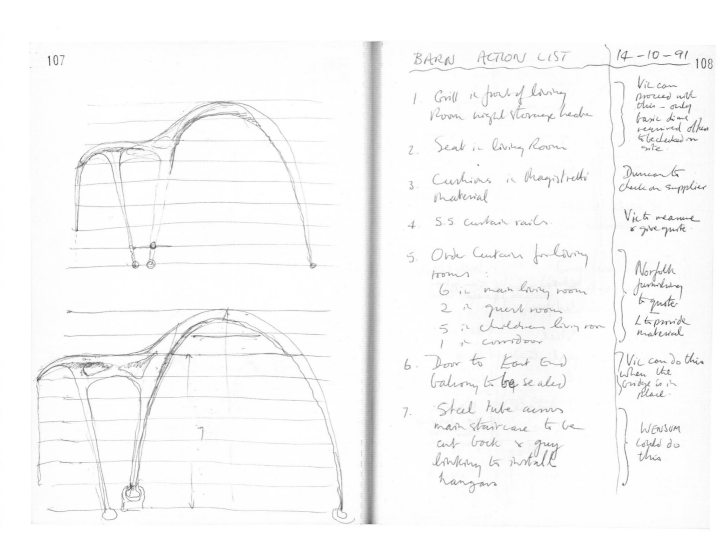

Ludwig Erhard Haus, Berlin

Book 26, pages 84–5
18 December 1991

A more developed structure showing a vertebra with large and small arches from which hanging office floors are suspended.

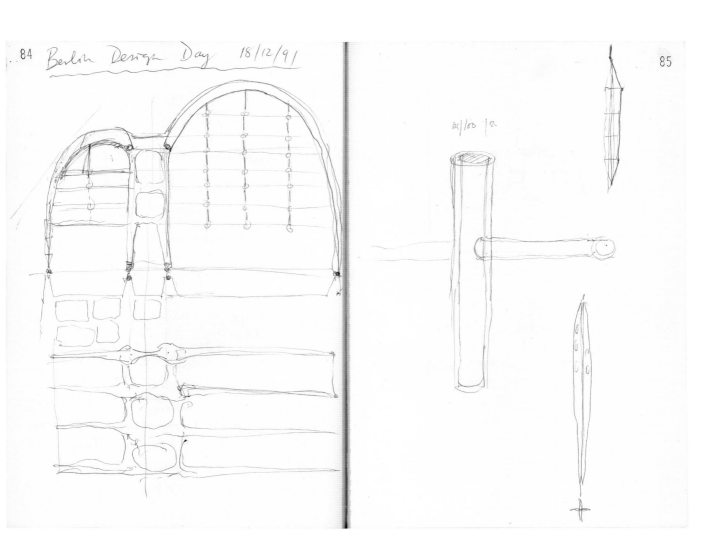

84   Berlin Design Day   18/12/91

85

Eurotunnel, Folkestone

Book 27, pages 16–17
Early March 1992

On the right is an early sketch for a 'left-over' site west of the huge Eurotunnel complex. The central building was completed and sits a little like a beacon or lighthouse at the edge of the site. People in the building (in which ticket sales are administered) have a panoramic view of vehicles driving onto the trains, and drivers can orientate themselves with a key building.

16

- Eurotunnels Dev's are separate to Eurotunnel
- Different requirement for their building.
- Tele-ticket sales – virtually all their space
- A.C. – like fresh air.
- Pre-funded:
  Integrated approach.
  - residential, shopping distribution, offices.
- Views from where they get out of their cars.
- A.A. or R.A.C
- Night-time views
- Landscaping.
  Kelsey Associates :–

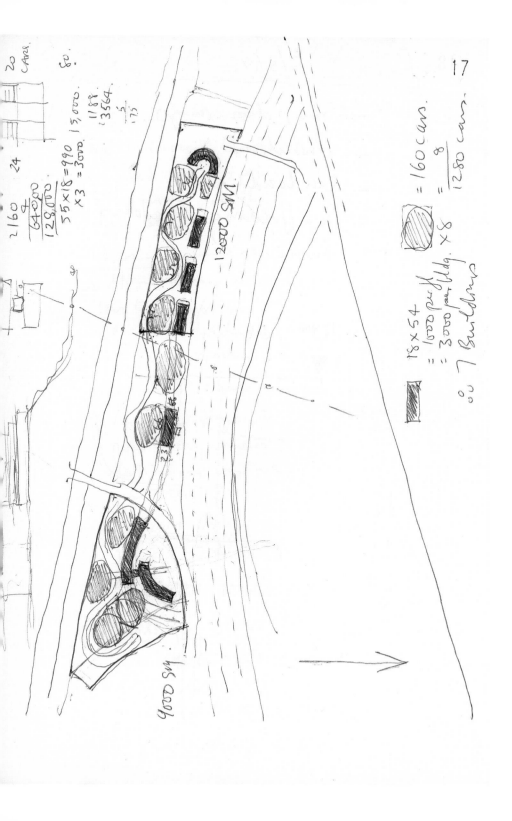

17

2 160
4
64,000
128,000

55×18 =990
×3 =3,000

15,000

1187
'3564

5
175

20
cars.

24

80.

12,000 SM

9000 SM

18×54
=1600 per fl
=3000 per bldg.
∴ 7 Buildings.

=160 cars.
×8
=1,280 cars.

A further development
showing a single arch
from which all floors
are suspended.

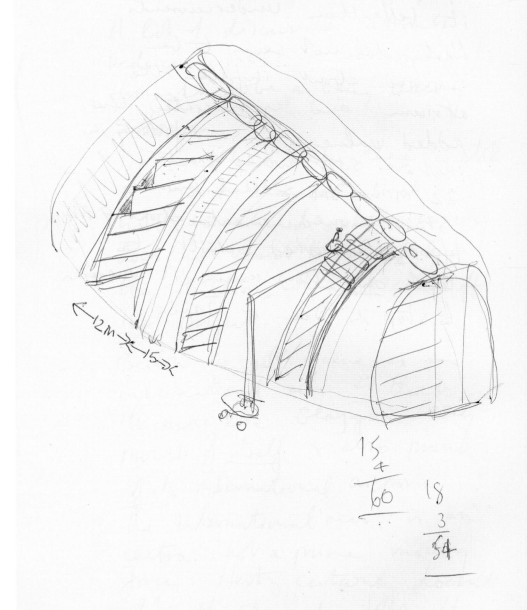

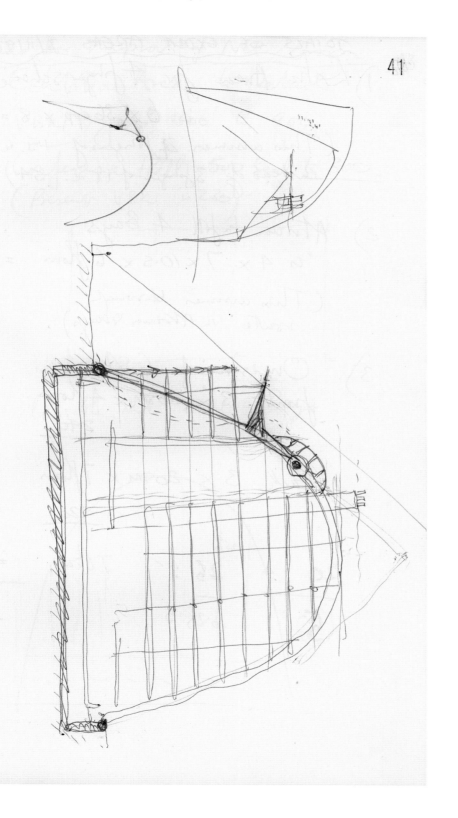

RAC Regional Headquarters, Bristol

Book 30, pages 38–9
Late March 1993

Early explorations of a building with an integrated parking area. On the right, initial thoughts for a building in the form of a free-standing pod.

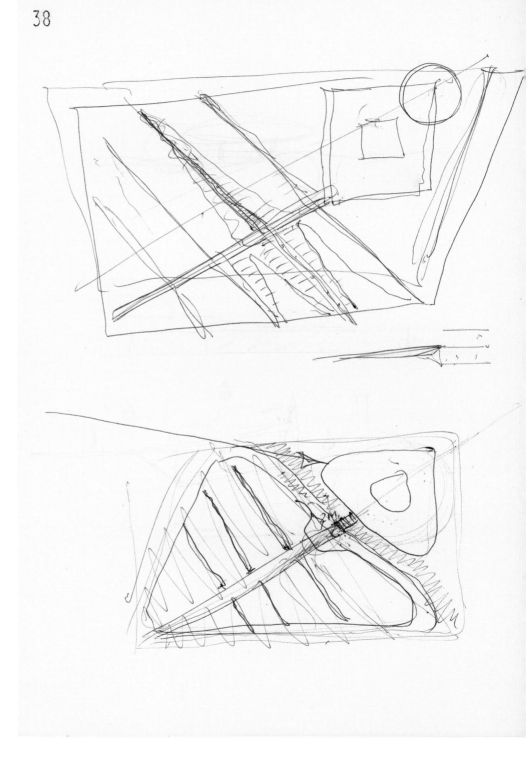

38

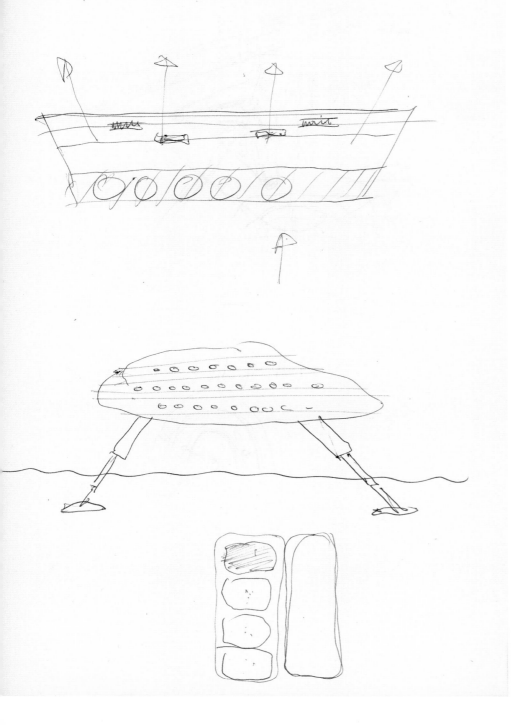

Ludwig Erhard Haus,
Berlin

Book 31, pages 114–15
14 July 1993

Another illustration of
the Ludwig Erhard Haus
as a 'bony' structure. Here
the arch comes down into
a socket at ground level
with vertical elements
supporting the cladding
on the street façade.

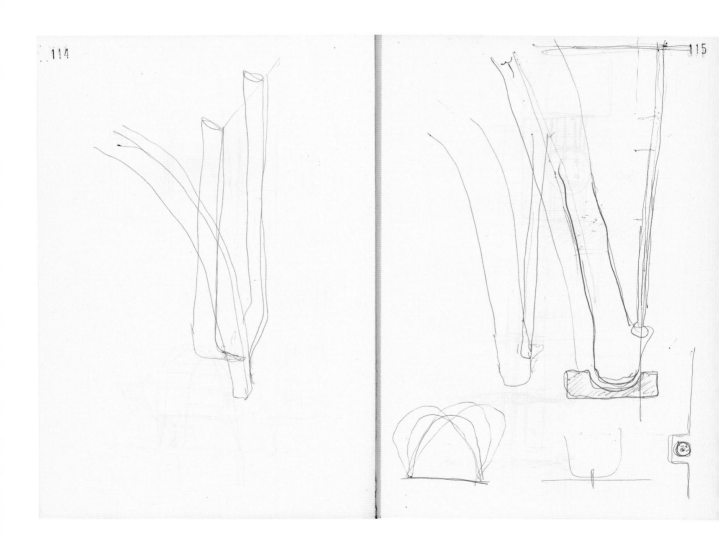

Bristol Millennium Project

Book 32, pages 46–7
Late September/early
October 1993

This idea for a concert hall shows a cocoon-like shape that sits inside an outer envelope. Giant pivoting doors not only allow access but can also be used to vary the acoustics. Some of these ideas were later picked up in the concert hall at EMPAC, New York (see Books 56–58).

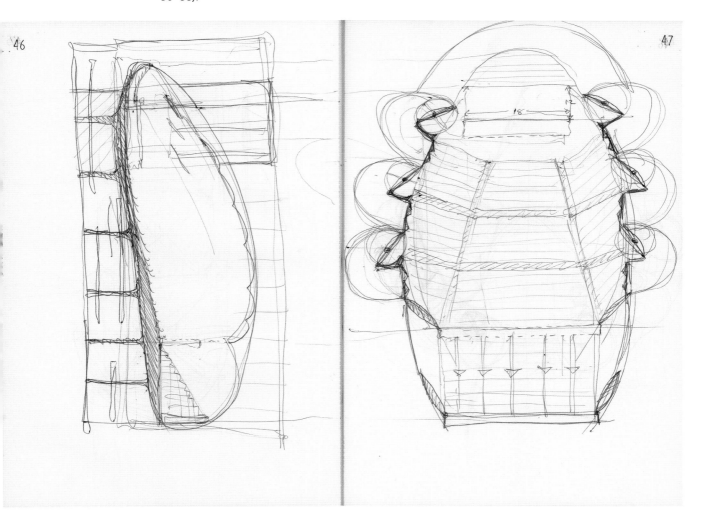

Ludwig Erhard Haus, Berlin

Book 32, pages 74–5
5 October 1993

This drawing explores the scale and shape of the huge 'feet' at the springing point of the arches which form the building's main structure. I always intended that these 'feet' should be seen by the public at street level so that the sheer power of the structure could be experienced.

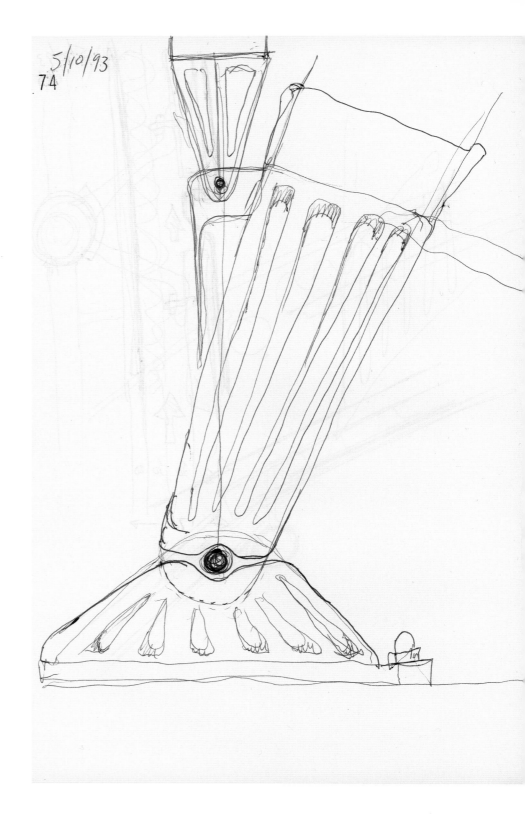

5/10/93
74

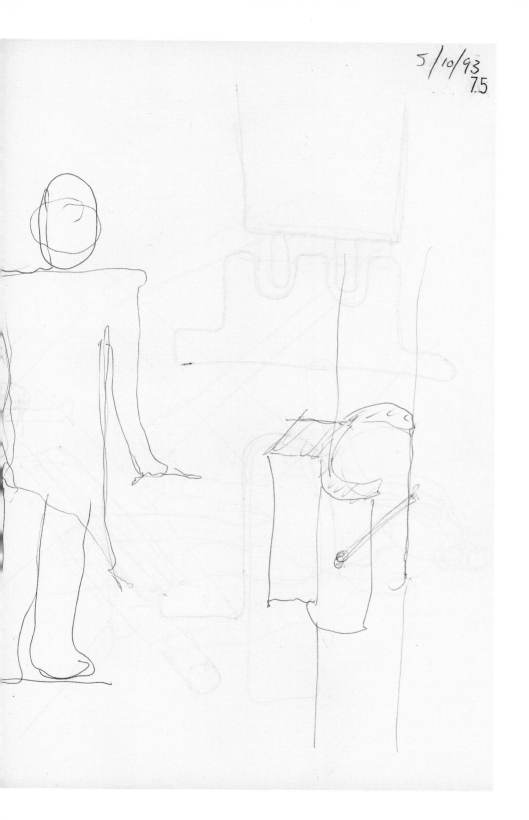

5/10/93
7.5

Lourdes Airport

Book 33, pages 6–6a
Late November 1993

A sketch for a roof structure for an airport competition. V-shaped beams carry all services with flat areas of roof between them.

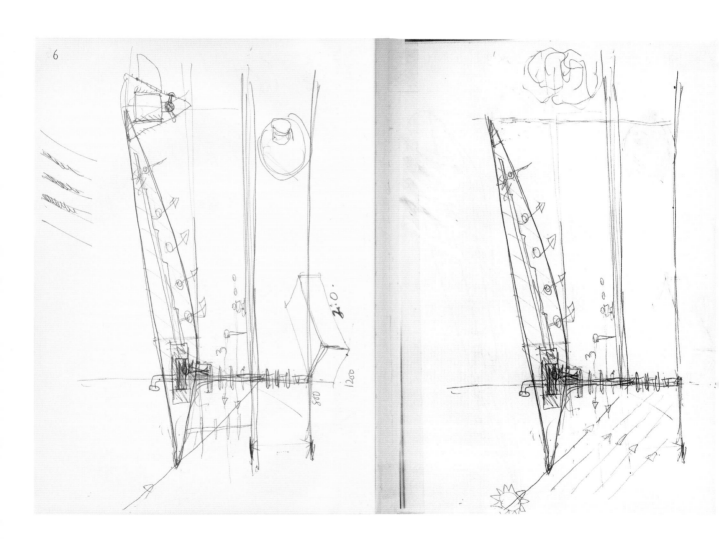

Lisbon Expo

Book 34, page 20
Late February 1994

An idea for the interchange between the railway and coach stations. I was exploring the central entrance hall and relating it to one of those mermaid's purse fish-egg cases commonly found on the beach.

Office building, Vienna

Book 34, page 129
c. June 1994

I believe this is an early sketch for a competition for a large office building in Vienna. The concept is to have the offices in a free-form strip, inside a rectilinear glazed enclosure housing a virtual forest.

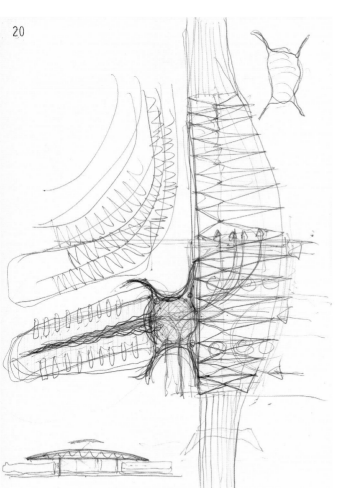

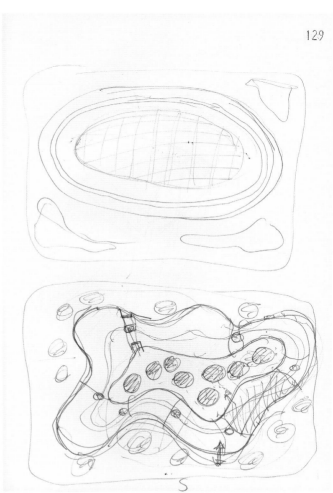

Work station

Book 35, pages 32–3
Early July 1994

This plan view shows all the facilities arranged around a vertical structure whose height is the same as a person standing with their arms stretched above them. On the right, some notes for Heathrow Terminal 3.

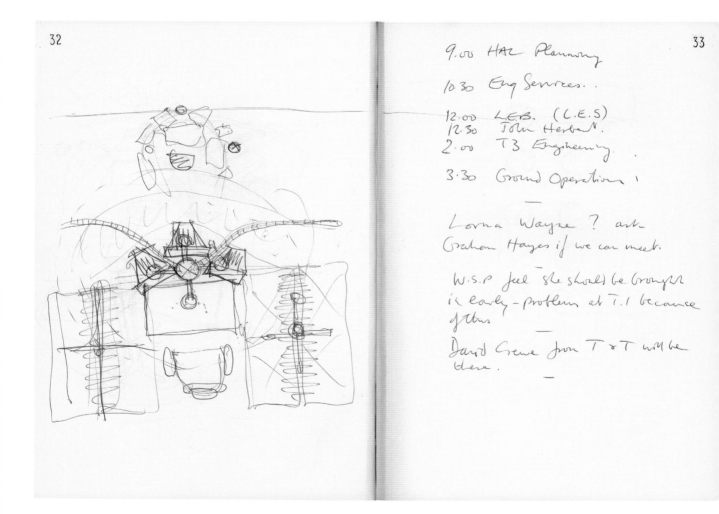

32

33

9.00 HAL Planning

10.30 Eng Services..

12.00 L.E.B. (L.E.S)
12.30 John Herbert.
2.00 T3 Engineering. .

3.30 Ground Operations.

—

Lorna Wayne ? ask
Graham Hayes if we can meet.

W.S.P feel she should be brought
in early — problem at T.1 because
of this
—
David Crewe from T & T will be
there.
—

The Assembly Plant was
built in 1976 and this
sketch of the cladding
system was done from
memory. It shows how,
for reasons of economy,
a steel tube was used
structurally to support
an aluminium extrusion.
This in turn held the 6 mm
flanges of an insulated
panel secured by
a neoprene gasket.
On the left, some notes
for the International
Terminal at Waterloo.

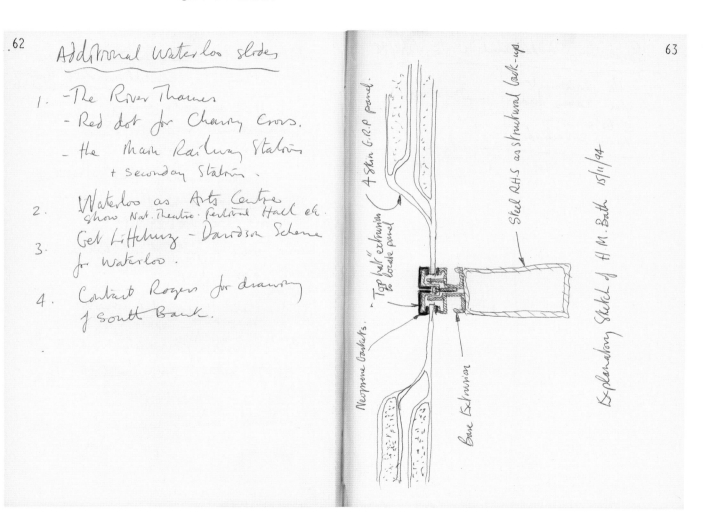

62

Additional Waterloo slides

1. - The River Thames
   - Red dot for Charing Cross.
   - the Main Railway Station
     + Secondary Station.

2. Waterloo as Arts Centre
   show Nat. Theatre· Festival Hall etc.

3. Get Lifschutz – Davidson Scheme
   for Waterloo.

4. Contact Rogers for drawing
   of South Bank.

63

4 Skin G.R.P panel.

Steel RHS as structural back-up.

"Top hat" extrusion
to locate panel

Neoprene Gaskets.

Base Extrusion

Explanatory Sketch of H.M.Bath 15/11/94

Park Road Apartments, London

Book 38, pages 36–7
30 April 1995

The drawings for 125 Park Road were made between 1968 and 1970 and unfortunately no longer exist. In order to illustrate the scheme in the book *Architecture, Industry and Innovation* I had to do this sketch from memory.

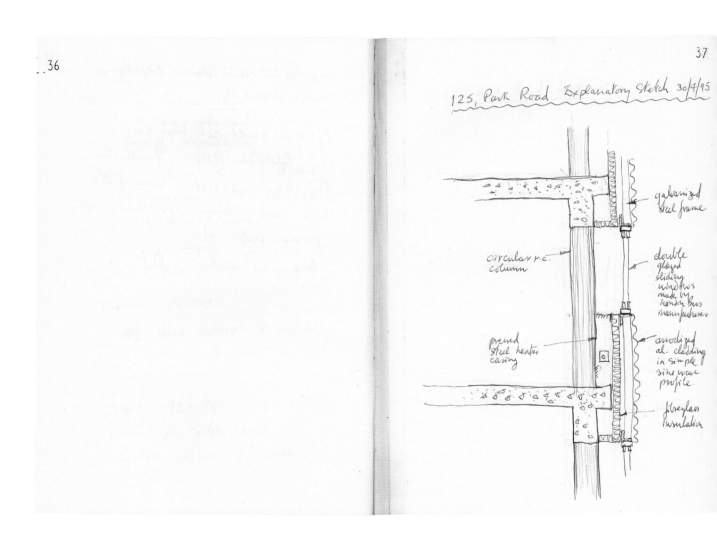

36

37

125, Park Road Explanatory Sketch 30/4/95

galvanized steel frame

circular r.c. column

double glazed sliding windows made by london bus manufacturer

pressed steel heater casing

anodized al. cladding in simple sine wave profile.

fibreglass insulation

**Heathrow Airport,
London**

Book 39, pages 50–1
c. September 1995

An early idea for a pier
using a lattice structure,
based on earlier work on
Heathrow Terminal 1,
Pier 4a.

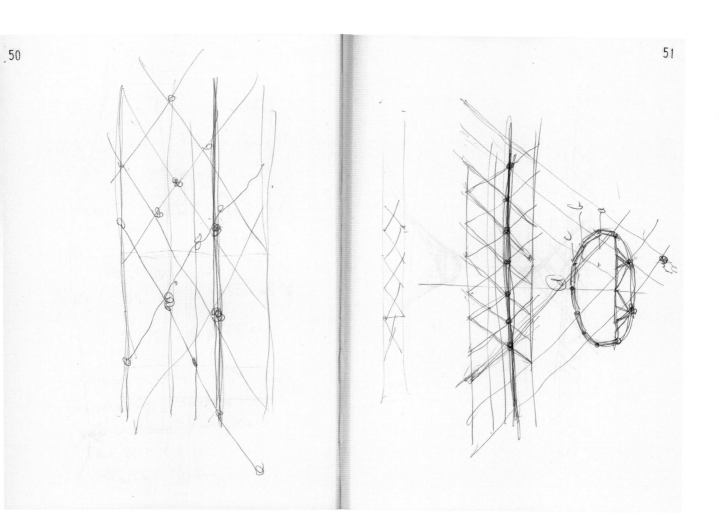

50

51

Designs for seating

Book 40, pages 136–7
12 March 1996

A sketch for a sofa made
using an elliptical
aluminium tube onto
which aluminium castings
are bolted.

136

SOFA : 12/3/96

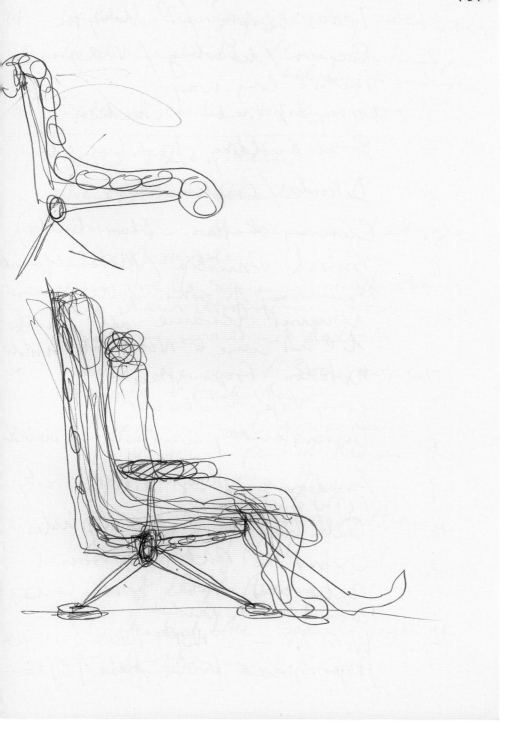

This exploratory sketch
shows the idea of leaning
trusses against the
planted rock face of the
quarry. The cladding area
is reduced by an earth
bank that conceals
concrete piloti, which in
turn support the arched
trusses. On the left, notes
for Lièges TGV station.

88 Tel Con with Michael Blaye 12·45 11/

Michael Blaye

Lieges.   TGV Station.

Deadline   June 19th:

Shortlist : of 5.

Leading Architect...

Privately Operating Corporation

French Trust on Tender.

— Try Alan Stauver
— Svenden hall . Ambassador.
— Architects Journal.

Mtg @ Heligan   12/6/96

_ 400 letters to written of support.

_

1) Management Structure (A Richard)
                              Branson

2) Safety or Cash Issues (Cut back costs)
   Bunker Case / Restaurants
   Shops

3) Cut Back Strategy if Common
   Market does not produce.

Zurich Airport

Book 41, page 5
16 April 1996

Book 43, page 121
c. February 1997

Explorations of a
basic wing shape formed
from two ellipses.

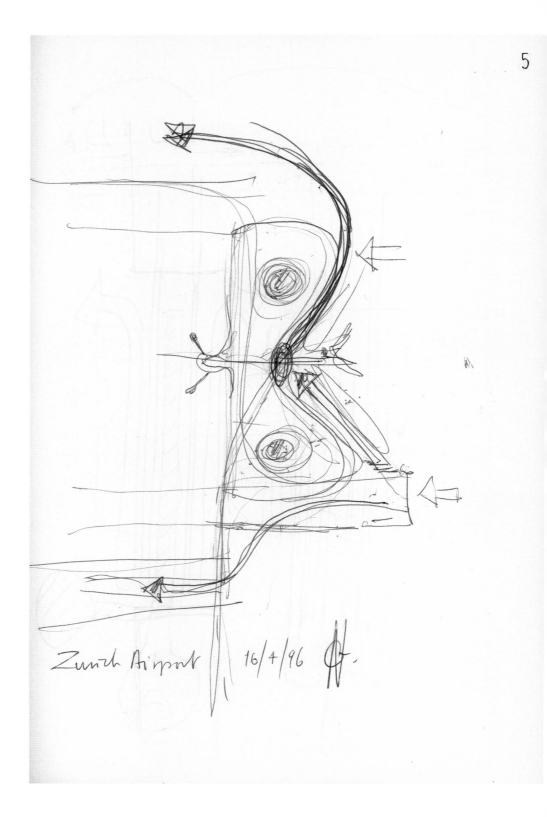

Zurich Airport | 16/4/96

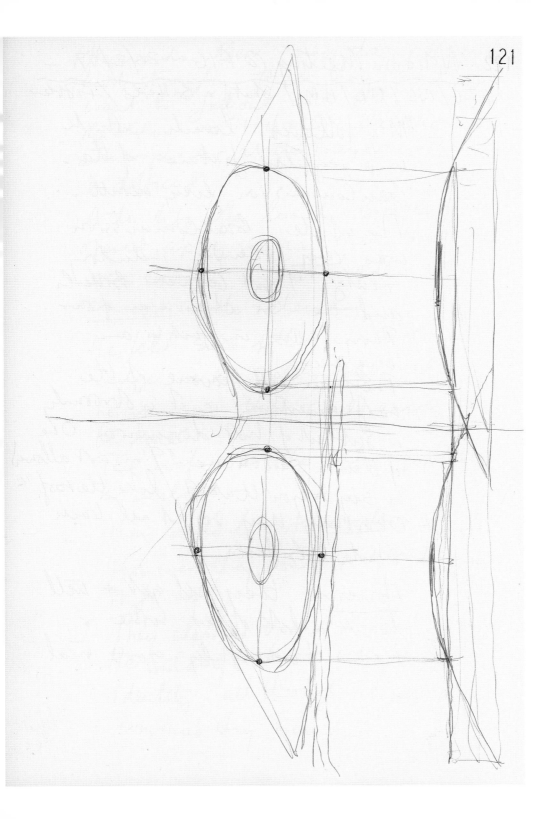

Village Hall, Burnham Market, Norfolk

Book 42, pages 136–7
Early October 1996

A central spine supports perforated plywood beams held up by props at their ends. The whole assemblage did perhaps become a little too fish-like in the end.

136

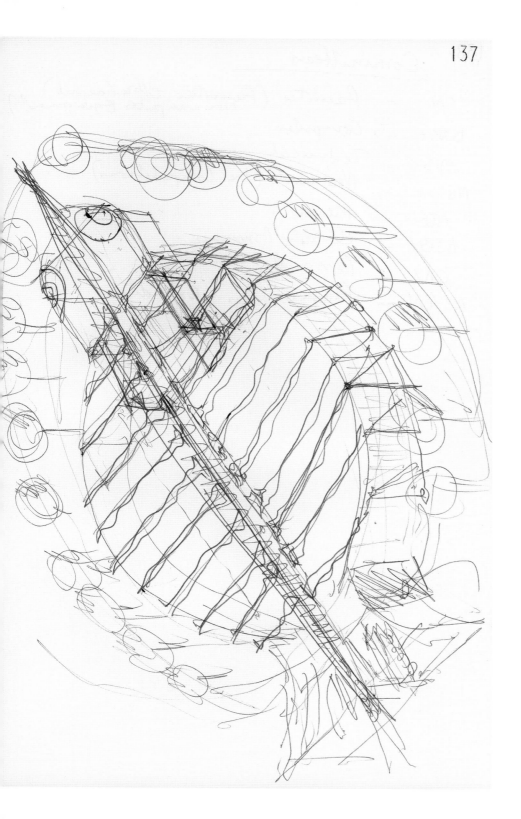

A plan view showing how
each room is attached to
the spine and that each
has a small outdoor
courtyard landscaped in
a different way.

Door handles

Book 44, pages 108–9
c. June 1997

These door handles were designed so that wooden or plastic surfaces of various types and colours could be applied to them. They went into production with FSB but only with black plastic surfaces.

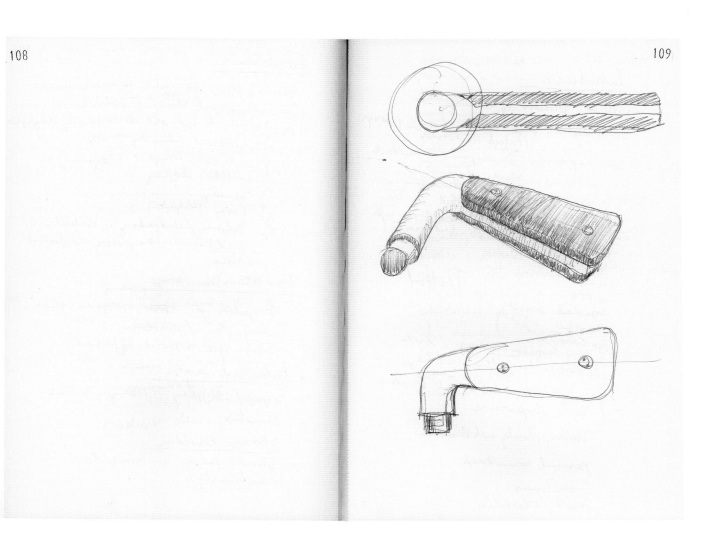

Eden Project, St Austell

Book 45, pages 106–7
c. September 1997

An early sketch
emphasising the need for
a major channel between
the domes in order to
collect as much rainwater
as possible for irrigating
the plants.

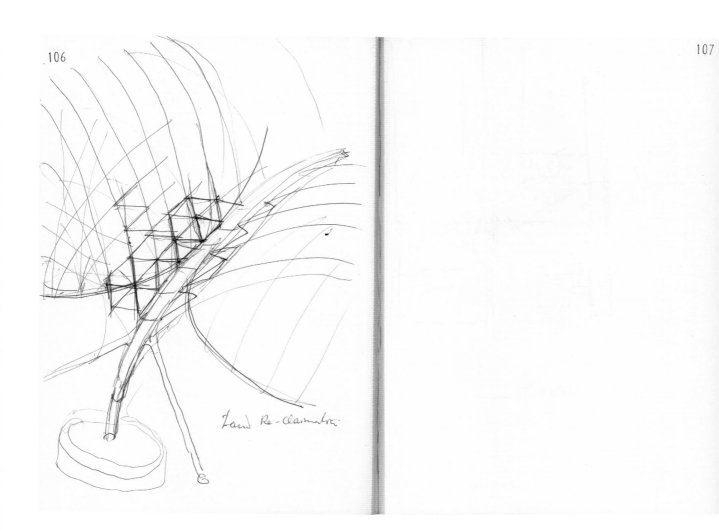

106

107

Land Re-Claimation

Eden Project, St Austell

Book 46, pages 16–17
c. November 1997

A drawing showing a
delicate arched structure
supporting the roof and a
major service access at the
mid-point of the slope.

16

435 — 1133   £ 355.

17

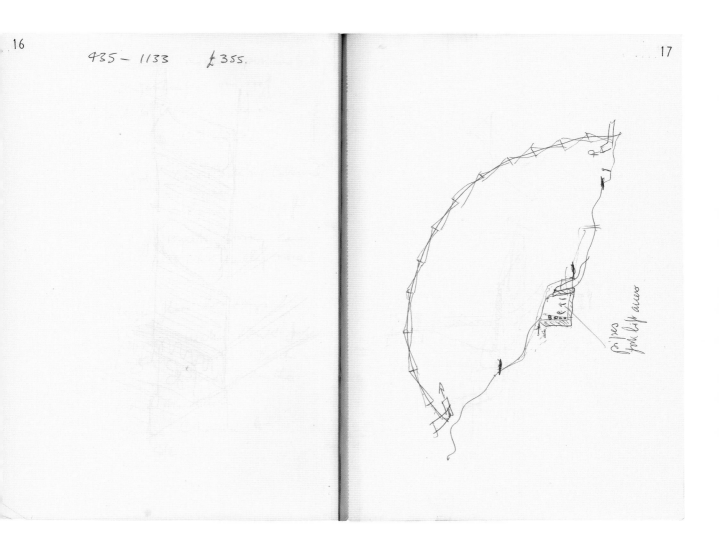

Minerva Tower/
St Botolphs, London

Book 47, pages 4–4a
Late January/early February 1998

The area of this open-plan office building amounted to about 450,000 square feet. The idea in the preliminary sketch on the right is to keep all the lifts and stairs on the periphery and to allow the skin of the building to follow the site boundary. On the left, a calculation that the scheme could be replaced by a 26-floor tower block. The project was later superseded by an alternative scheme for the same client, known as St Botolphs.

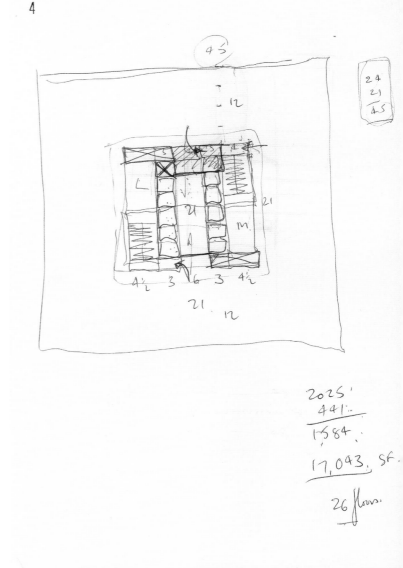

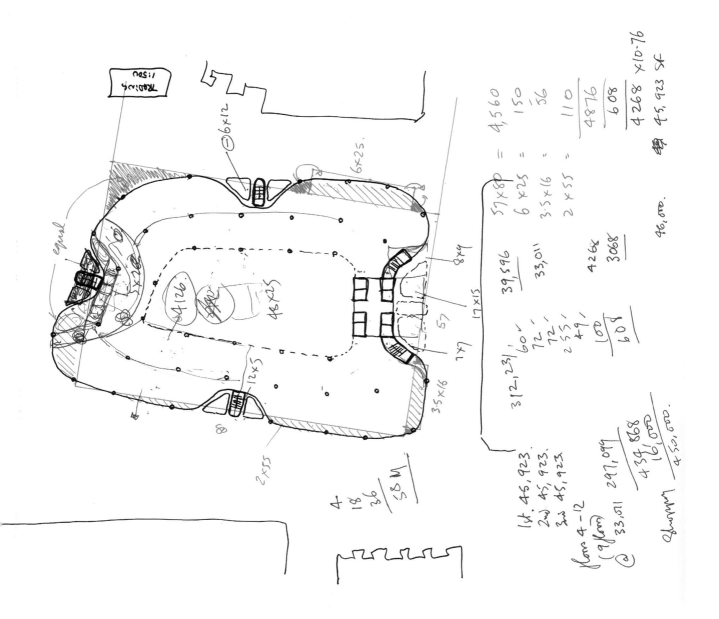

Spine House, Cologne

Book 48, pages 100–1
c. June 1998

An early drawing
envisaging the house
with a 'fuselage' spine.
The entrance is at one
end, while at the other
a cockpit offers
panoramic views of
the countryside.

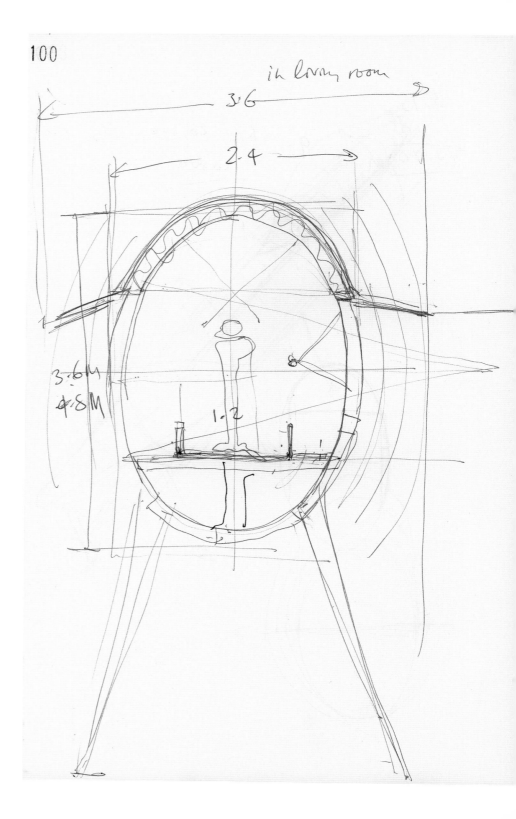

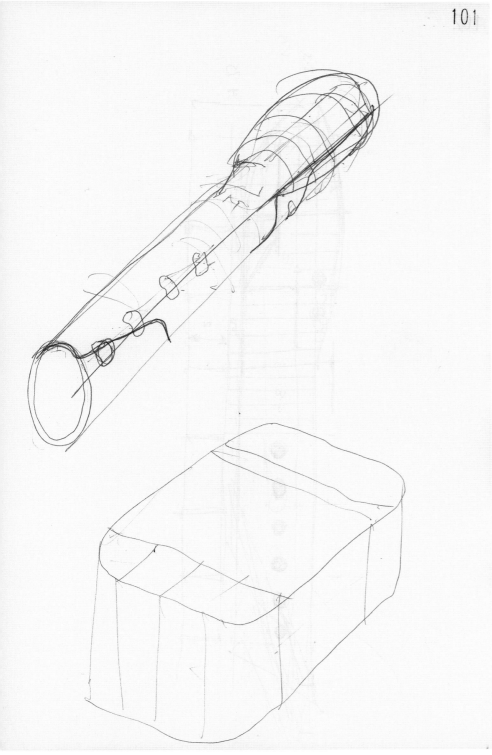

Thermae Bath Spa

Book 48, pages 120–1
8 July 1998

This early sketch shows a large hot bath at basement level with the main supporting columns for the structure passing through it. The columns extend throughout the whole building and support the rooftop pool. The whole of the 'solid' stone and clad structure is enclosed in an outer glass skin to provide climate control.

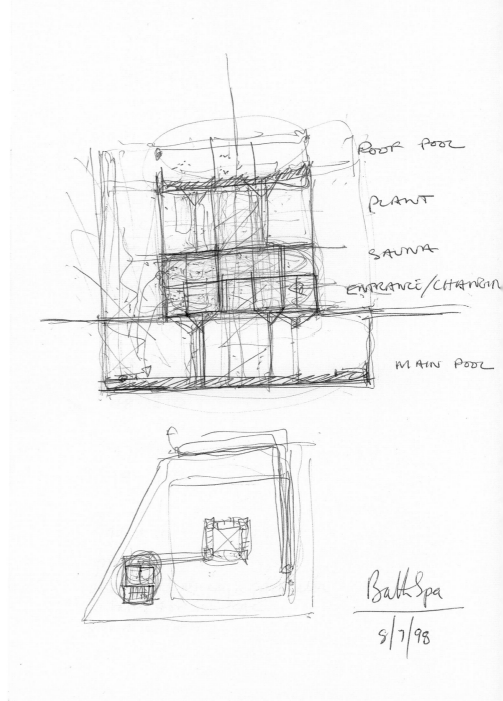

120

ROOF POOL

PLANT

SAUNA

ENTRANCE/CHANGIN

MAIN POOL

Bath Spa
8/7/98

QA Meeting 9/7/98

- QI's a Management System.
  not just a quality system

- 9001   has 20 principles   25%
  9002   has 19   "   66%
  9003   has 12   "   9%

- So Archs in UK are QA registered.
- We need ISO 14000 as well.
- Who Champions the system.
  Company Manual / Project Manual

- "Does it affect the way you
  service your clients."

**De Young Museum,
San Francisco**

Book 49, pages 110–11
14 December 1998

This was a first thought
for a competition for the
museum. A central spine
follows the contours of
the site and each gallery
has a 'shop window'
looking out to entice
visitors inside.

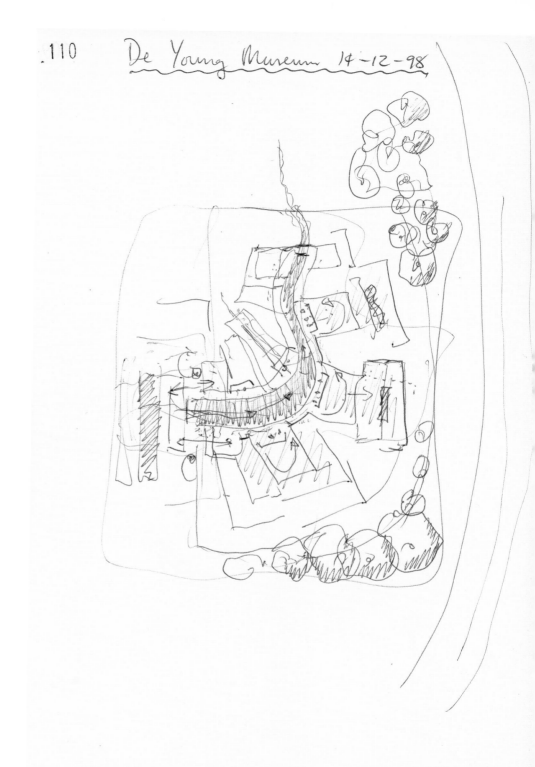

_110   De Young Museum 14-12-98

- Slides from John Ellis
- Katherine Gustaffson.
- Burrell Collection slides
- Shopwindow idea.
- Slides of CEH & Waterloo
- Rammed Earth Wood.
- Grass Roof
- Western Morning News night-time.
- Western Morning News interior.
- Emphasize Chinese influences.
- Corbusier's Carpenter Centre.

Frankfurt Trade Fair Hall

Book 51, pages 10–11
c. May 1999

First thoughts for
a wide-spanning roof.
The idea is to use curving
leaf-like structures that
interlock to form a
homogenous roof.

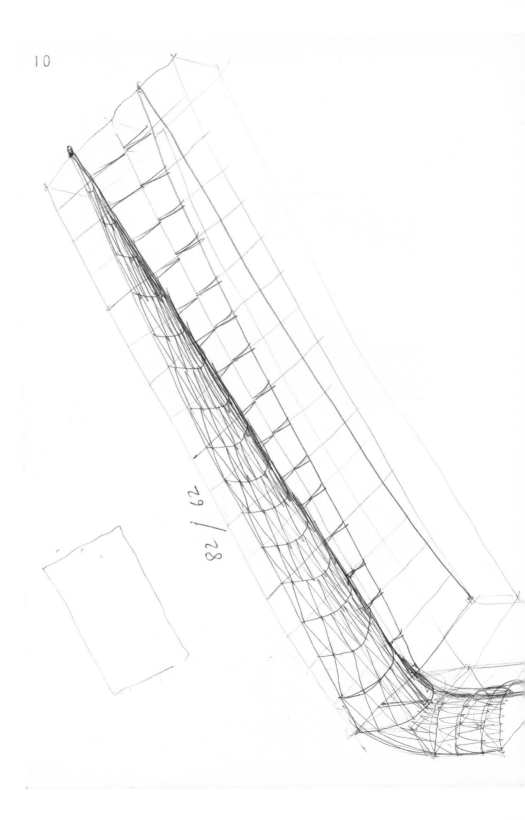

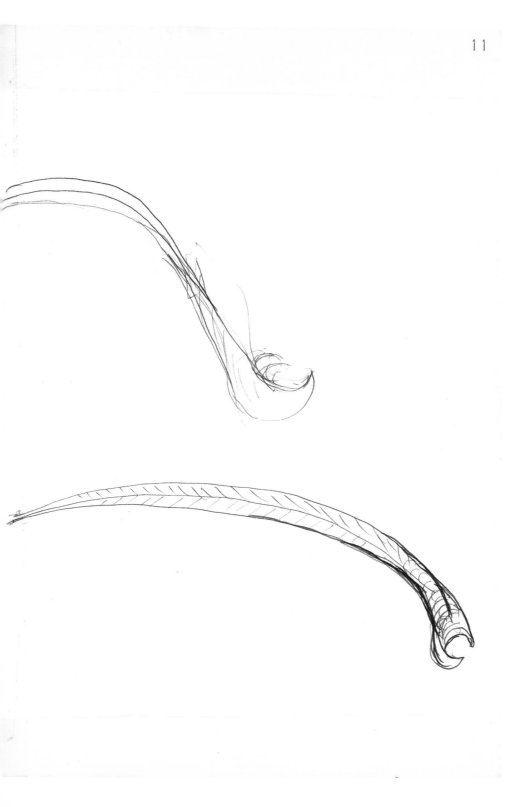

Frankfurt Trade Fair Hall

Book 52, pages 66–7
c. August 1999

In these further explorations I was thinking about curved vaulted arches with hanging roof elements between them. They are very similar to the final result.

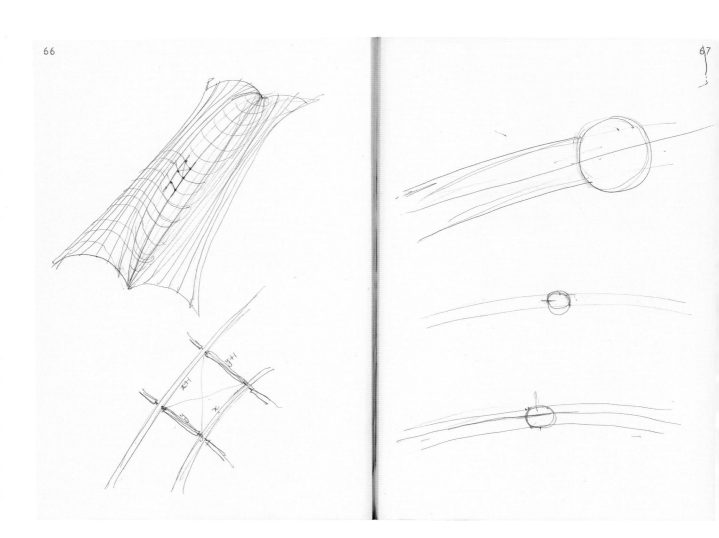

66

67

The idea for this simple
street seat is a steel tube,
onto which are bolted
one-piece stamped-out
steel seating shells. The
tube itself is supported
by 'elephant's foot'
pressings.

26

"The Elephant System"

The Press metal seat.
BURRI —— Zurich Trams might
make them.
20 DM.
1,000,000
60,000

27

Royal College of Art, London

Book 53, page 144a
15 May 2000

An ellipse was used to contrast with the existing rectilinear building and to echo the curving façade of the neighbouring Royal Albert Hall. A circulation tower between the two buildings formed the new entrance and acted as a 'mixing valve'.

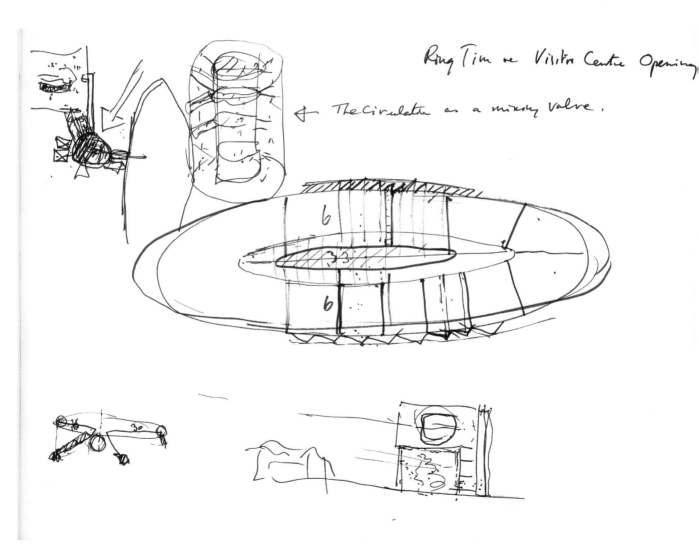

Ring Tim re Visitor Centre Opening

The Circulation as a mixing valve.

Zurich Airport

Book 54, pages 29–30
2 June 2000

Early sketches for the roof in which deep-spanning V-shaped trusses house all services. The trusses are simply supported on the landside and have a large overhang on the airside to block the sun from the south.

29

Zurich Airport Review 2 — 6 — 2000

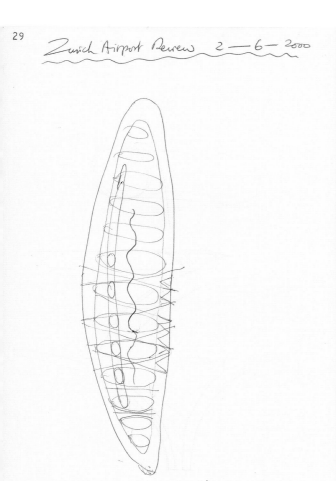

30

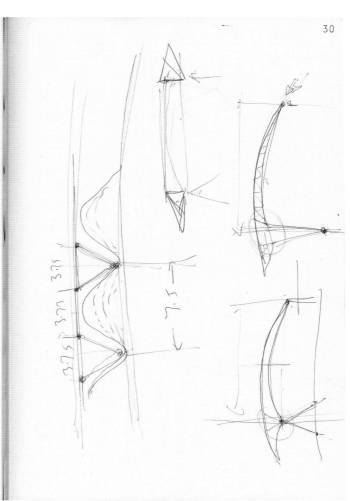

Experimental Media and Performing Arts Center, Troy, New York State

Book 56, pages 144–5
25 March 2001

I made these drawings immediately after the briefing and site visit. At this stage I envisaged the concert hall 'floating' above a pedestrian level with the black boxes beneath it. The slope of the hill is used to form a natural amphitheatre.

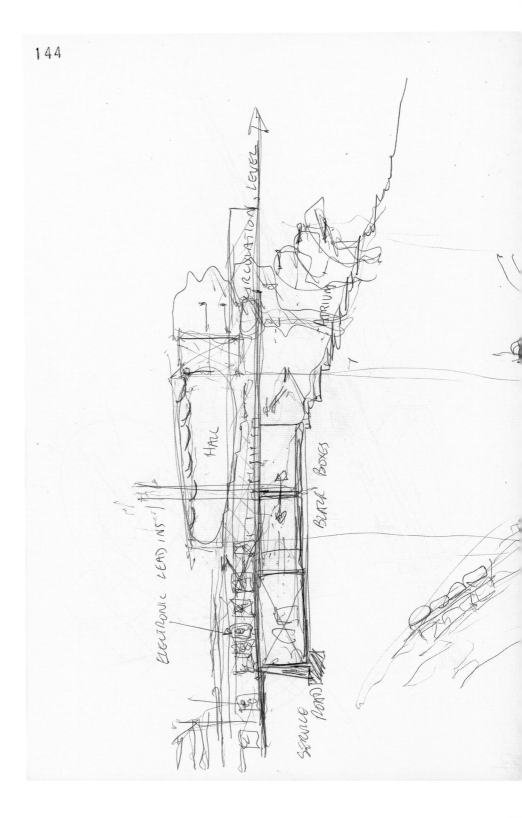

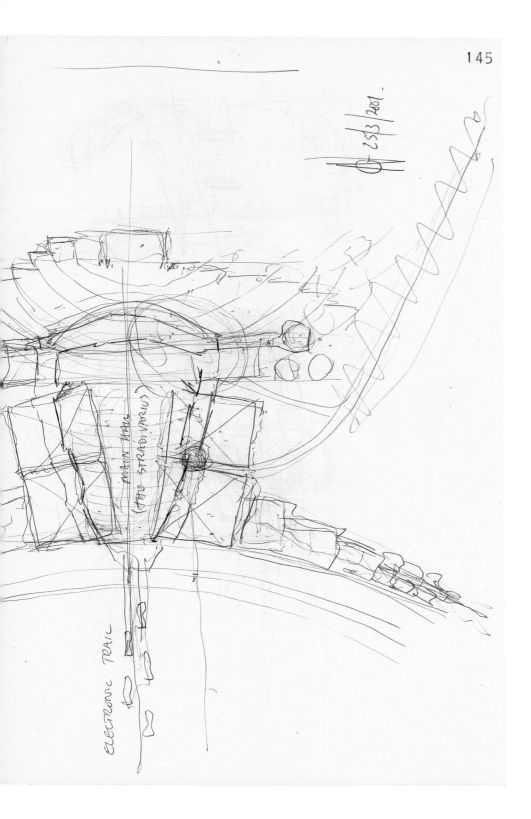

ELECTRONIC TRAIL

MAIN HALL
(THE STRADIVARIUS)

25/3/2001.

145

Experimental Media and
Performing Arts Center,
Troy, New York State

Book 57, pages 70–1
25 June 2001

The idea in these initial
concepts was to create
a large concert-hall space
and a smaller theatre
space by rotating a
curved shape around
a circulation datum.

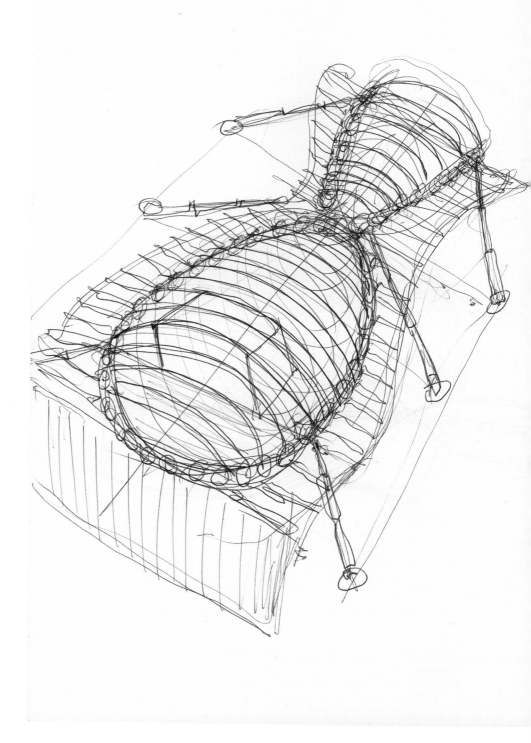

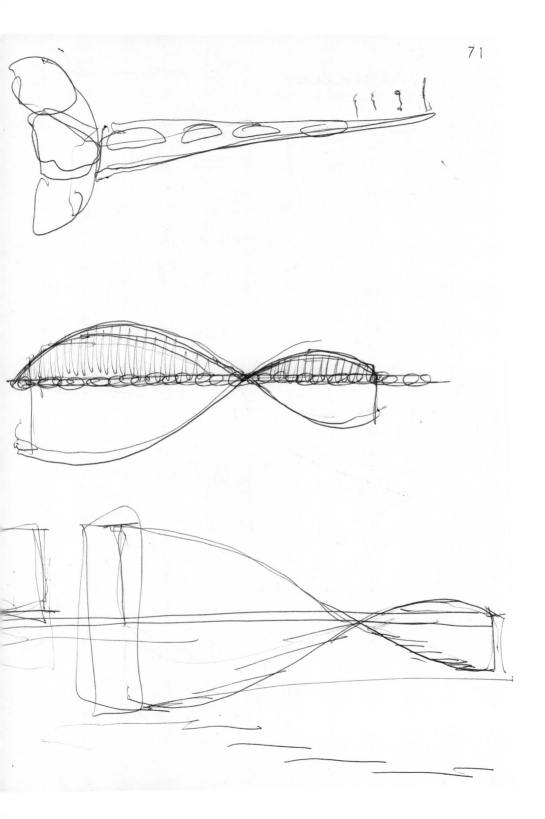

Experimental Media and
Performing Arts Center,
Troy, New York State

Book 58, pages 16a and 19a
23 October 2001

A later concept drawing
showing the theatre
backed by a huge
retaining wall and the
concert hall standing on
legs above a massive
cathedral-like
bar/reception/entertain-
ment space. The theatre,
concert hall and two

studios all face onto
a large entrance space,
level with the campus.

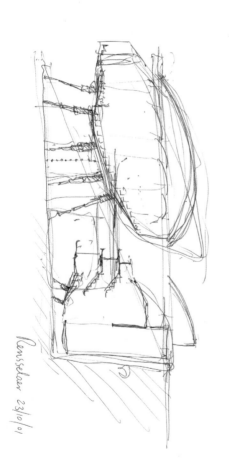

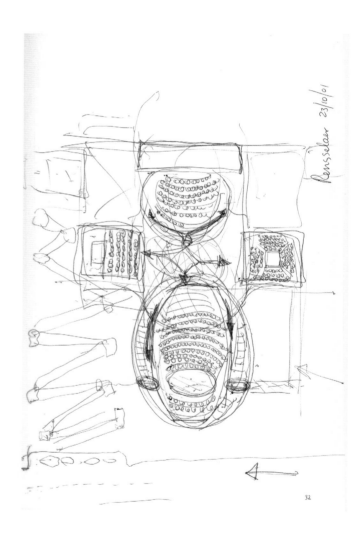

Eden Project, St Austell

Book 59, pages 64–5
21 February 2003

Phase 5 of the Eden Project is planned as a cable net-structure holding ETFE pillows. Here I was exploring the idea of joining two pillows edge to edge and avoiding a cold bridge.

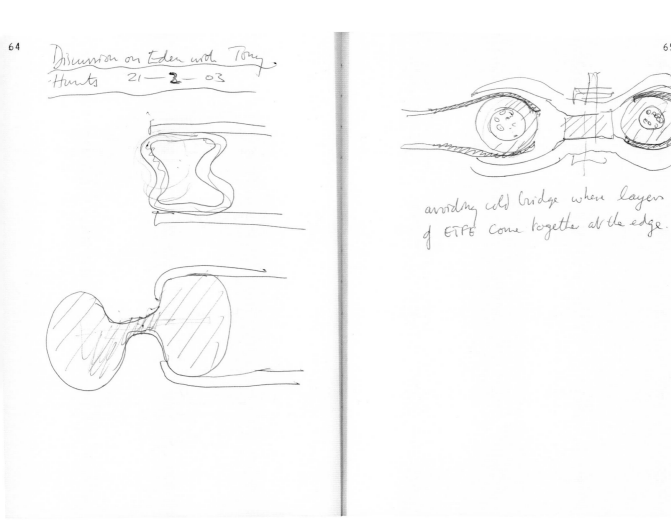

64

Discussion on Eden with Tony Hunts 21 — 2 — 03

65

avoiding cold bridge where layers of ETFE come together at the edge.

Copenhagen Bridge

Book 60, pages 136–7
11 May 2004

In these sketches for
the pedestrian bridge
a mega-structure passes
over the supports with
a telescopic central tube
that slides landwards like
a piston withdrawing
when access is needed
for ships.

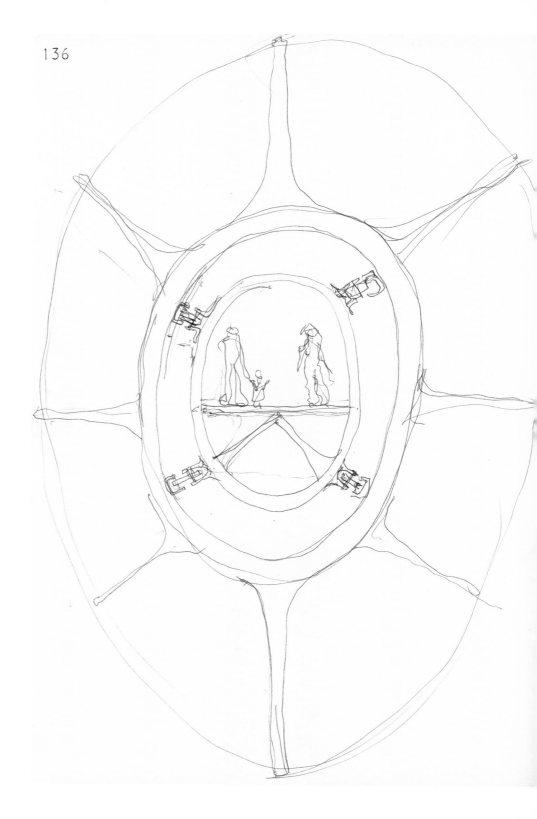

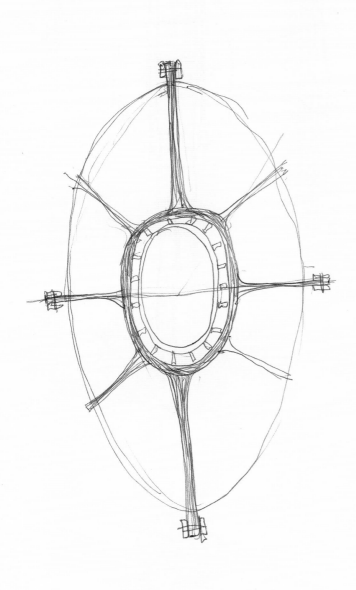

Copenhagen Bridge

Book 61, pages 24–5
c. May 2004

The bridge required
a pedestrian/cycle link
across the harbour with
as low a profile as
possible and one opening
section for ships to pass
through. The idea here is
an L-shaped structure that
rolls through 90 degrees –
a form of bascule bridge.

Swinging chair

Book 62, pages 120–1
End of 2006/early 2007

A concept for a garden swing-seat with a canopy that can be unrolled to protect the seat from the weather when it is not in use.

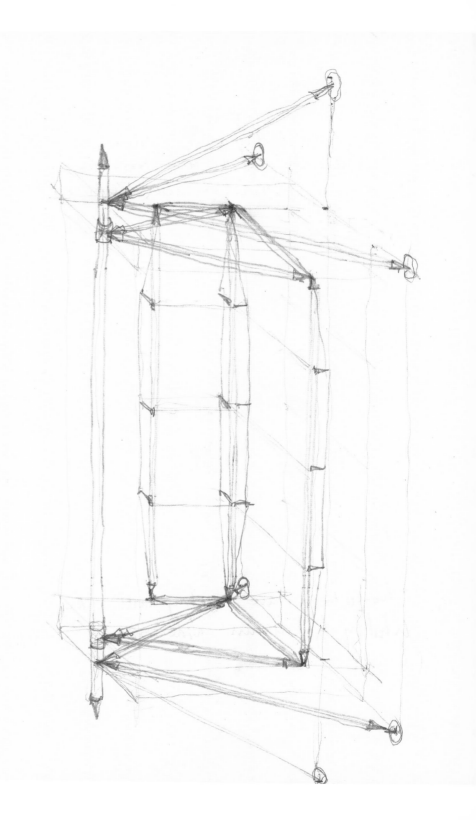

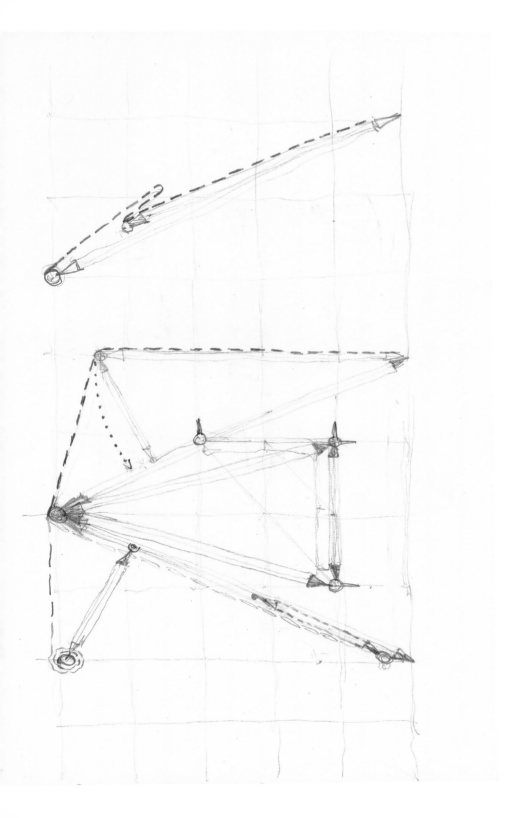

Pulkovo Airport, St Petersburg

Book 63, pages 42–3
Late May/early June 2007

In this early sketch of the roof, the shapes are based on the idea of retaining the snow as insulation and allowing it to melt slowly *in situ*. Small roof lights allow shafts of low winter sunlight to reflect from small gold areas within the roof space.

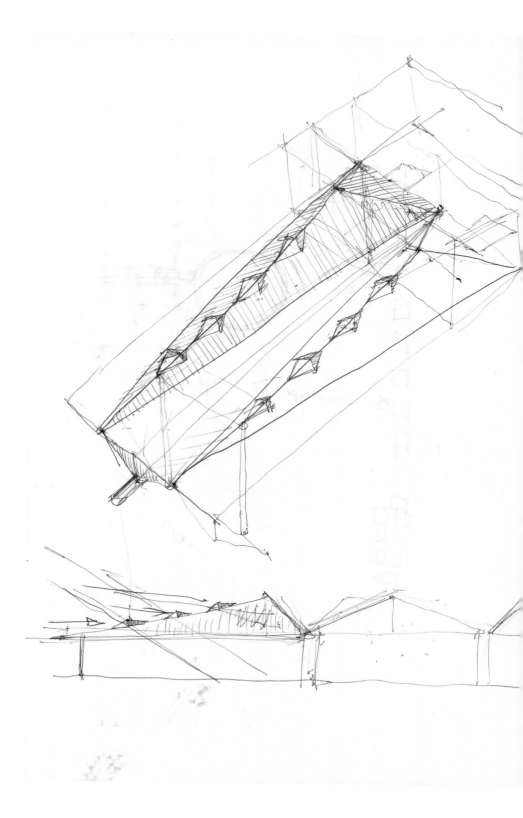

ST. PETERSBURG – Influences

- Low Sun (glints)
- Snow / Ice
- Gold.
- Hot Summer / Cold Winter.
- Water.
- White Columns.!
- Arches !
- Rainwater pipes.
- Windows !
  daylight v. heat loss
- Bridges / Islands.

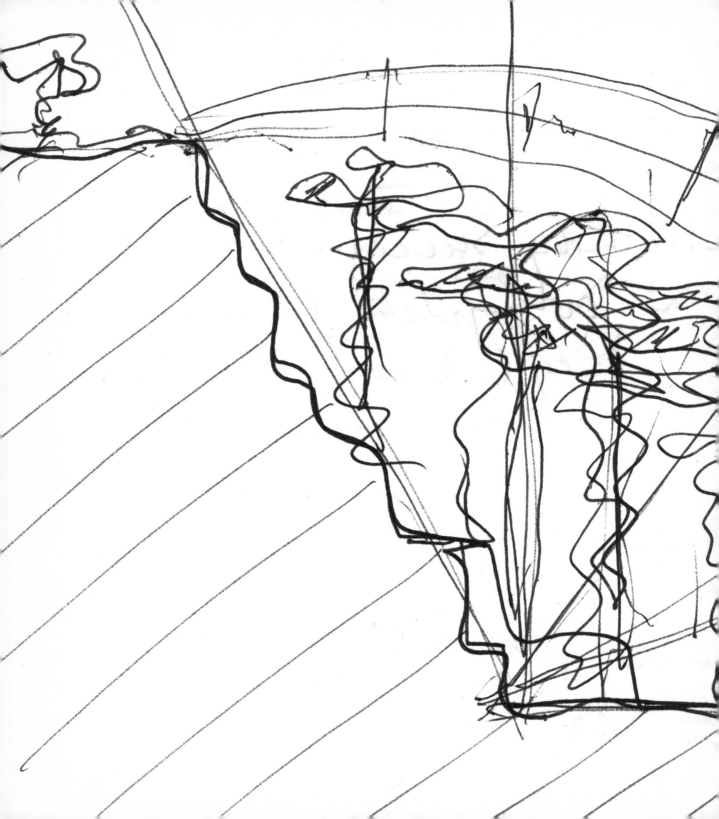

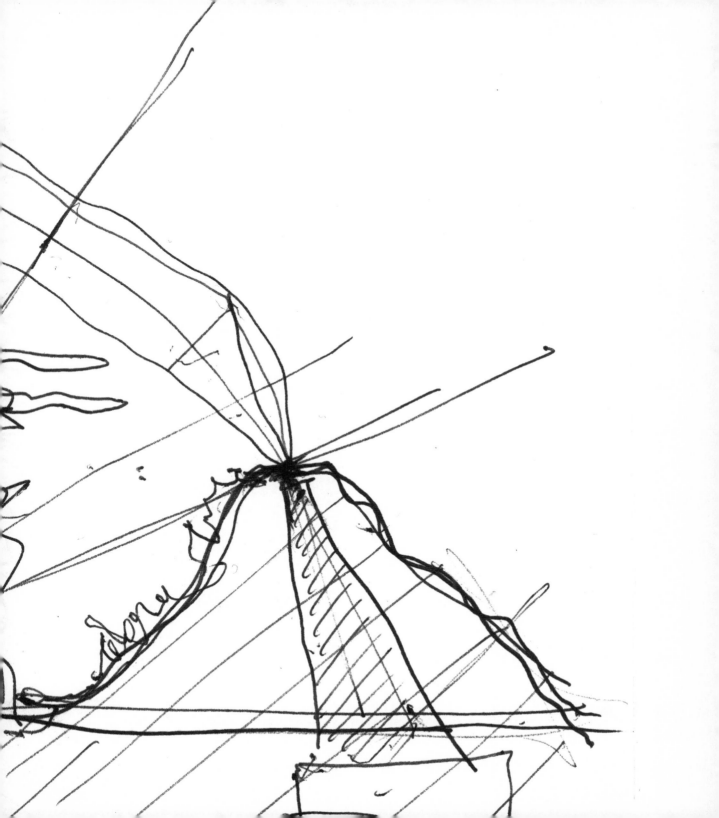

SELECTED PHOTOGRAPHS

These projects, arranged in chronological order by start
date, all relate to sketches reproduced in this book.

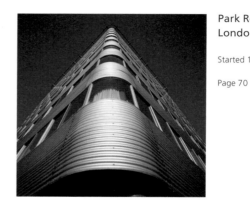

**Park Road Apartments,
London**

Started 1968; completed 1970

Page 70

**Herman Miller
Assembly Plant, Bath**

Started and completed 1976

Page 69

**Herman Miller
Distribution Centre,
Chippenham**

Started 1982; completed 1983

Pages 18–19

Oxford Ice Rink

Started 1983; completed 1984

Pages 22–3, 25

Financial Times Print Works, London

Started 1986; completed 1988

Pages 30–1

Sainsbury's Superstore, Camden Town, London

Started 1985; completed 1988

Page 28

International Terminal Waterloo, London

Started 1988; completed 1993

Pages 34–7, 46–7

Homebase, Brentford, London

Started 1986; completed 1987

Page 29

Heathrow Terminal 5, London

Model made for competition 1989; project unrealised

Pages 42–3

Bibliothèque nationale, Paris

Model made for competition 1989; project unrealised

Page 44

Heathrow Terminal 1, Pier 4a, London

Started 1989; completed 1993

Page 71

Herman Miller Furniture System

Designed and realised 1989–1990

Page 45

Western Morning News Headquarters and Print Works, Plymouth

Started 1990; completed 1993

Pages 52–3

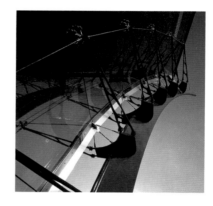

British Pavilion, Expo '92, Seville

Started 1989; completed 1992

Pages 38–41

Igus Factory, Cologne

Started 1990; ongoing

Pages 48–9

Ludwig Erhard Haus, Berlin

Started 1991; completed 1998

Pages 54–5, 58–9, 62, 64–5

Spine House, Cologne

Started 1996; completed 2002

Pages 80, 86–7

RAC Regional Headquarters, Bristol

Started 1993; completed 1994

Pages 60–1

Zurich Airport

Started 1996; completed 2004

Pages 76–7, 97

Eden Project, St Austell

Phase 1 started 1996; phase 2 completed 2001; ongoing

Pages 74–5, 82–3, 103

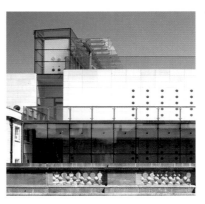

Thermae Bath Spa

Started 1997; completed 2006

Pages 88–9

Frankfurt Trade Fair Hall

Started 1999; completed 2001

Pages 92–4

St Botolphs, London

Started 2006; ongoing

Pages 84–5

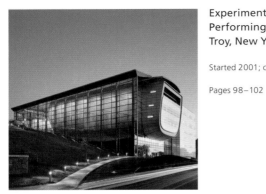

Experimental Media and Performing Arts Center, Troy, New York State

Started 2001; completed 2008

Pages 98–102

Pulkovo Airport, St Petersburg

Started 2007; ongoing

Pages 110–11

FURTHER READING

Colin Amery
Architecture, Industry and Innovation:
The Early Work of Nicholas Grimshaw & Partners,
Phaidon Press Limited, London, 1995

Rowan Moore (ed.)
Structure, Space and Skin:
The Work of Nicholas Grimshaw & Partners,
Phaidon Press Limited, London, 1993

Hugh Pearman
Equilibrium: The Work of Nicholas
Grimshaw & Partners,
Phaidon Press Limited, London, 2000

PHOTOGRAPHIC ACKNOWLEDGEMENTS

© Richard Bryant/ARCAID
British Pavilion, Expo '92, p. 116

© Peter Cook
International Terminal Waterloo, p. 115;
RAC Regional Headquarters, p. 117

© Michael Dyer Associates Ltd
Herman Miller Assembly Plant, p. 114; Bibliothèque
nationale, Herman Miller Furniture System, p. 116

© Grimshaw
Heathrow Terminal 1, Pier 4a, p. 116; Eden Project, p. 117;
St Botolphs, Pulkovo Airport, p. 118

© Werner Huthmacher
Ludwig Erhard Haus, pp. 12 (right), 117

© Waltraud Krase
Frankfurt Trade Fair Hall, p. 118

© Adam Parker
Eden Project, p. 14

© Jo Reid and John Peck
Oxford Ice Rink, pp. 12, 115; British Pavilion, Expo '92,
p. 14; Herman Miller Distribution Centre, p. 114;
Sainsbury's, p. 115; Homebase, p. 115; Financial Times
Print Works, p. 115; Igus Factory, p. 116

© Paúl Rivera/Archphoto
Experimental Media and Performing Arts Center, p. 118

© Peter Strobel
International Terminal Waterloo detail, p. 15;
Western Morning News, p. 116

© Edmund Sumner/VIEW
Frankfurt Trade Fair Hall, p. 13; Zurich Airport, pp. 13, 117;
Spine House, Thermae Bath Spa, p. 117

© Tessa Traeger
Service tower, p. 11; Park Road Apartments, p. 114

© Jens Willebrand
Ludwig Erhard Haus, p. 12 (centre); Heathrow Terminal 5,
p. 115

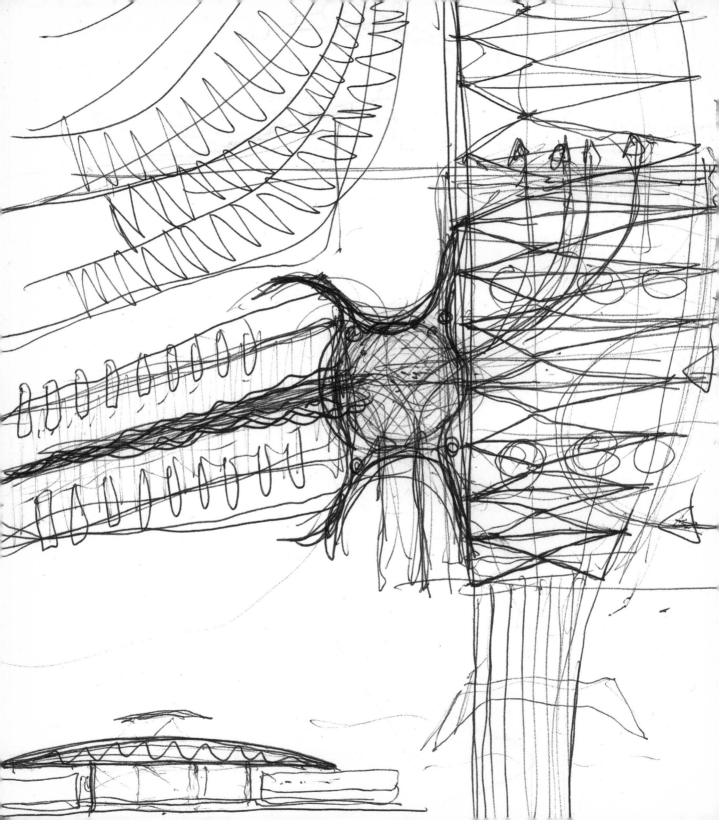